A-Z PETERB

G000277859

CONTEN

Key to Map Pages	2-3
Large Scale City Centre	4-5
Map Pages	6-31

Ind…	
Villa…	…J2-44
Selected Places of Interest	

REFERENCE

Motorway	**A1(M)**
A Road	**A15**
B Road	**B1091**
Dual Carriageway	
One-way Street	→
Traffic flow on A Roads is also indicated by a heavy line on the driver's left.	→
Road Junction Number	㊱
Restricted Access	
Pedestrianized Road	
Track & Footpath	
Residential Walkway	
Cycleway	
Railway	Level Crossing / Station
Heritage Railway	Station
Built-up Area	CHURCH LA.
Map Continuation	16	Large Scale City Centre 4
Local Authority Boundary	

Posttown Boundary	
Postcode Boundary (within Posttown)	
Car Park (Selected)	P
Church or Chapel	†
Fire Station	■
House Numbers A & B Roads only	22 / 10
Hospital	H
Information Centre	i
National Grid Reference	^{5}15
Police Station	▲
Post Office	★
Toilet: without facilities for the Disabled	▽
with facilities for the Disabled	▽
Educational Establishment	▭
Hospital or Hospice	▭
Industrial Building	▭
Leisure or Recreational Facility	▭
Place of Interest	▭
Public Building	▭
Shopping Centre or Market	▭
Other Selected Buildings	▭

SCALE

Map Pages 6-31   1:15840

0   ¼   ½ Mile
0   250   500   750 Metres
4 inches (10.16 cm) to 1 mile   6.31 cm to 1 km

Map Pages 4-5   1:7920

0   ⅛   ¼ Mile
0   100   200   300   400 Metres
8 inches (20.32cm) to 1 mile   12.63 cm to 1 km

Copyright of Geographers' A-Z Map Company Limited

Fairfield Road, Borough Green, Sevenoaks, Kent TN15 8PP
Telephone: 01732 781000 (Enquiries & Trade Sales)
01732 783422 (Retail Sales)
www.a-zmaps.co.uk

 Ordnance Survey® This product includes mapping data licensed from Ordnance Survey® with the permission of the Controller of Her Majesty's Stationery Office.
© Crown Copyright 2005. All rights reserved. Licence number 100017302

Copyright © Geographers' A-Z Map Co. Ltd.   Edition 3 2005, Edition 3A 2007 (Part Revision)

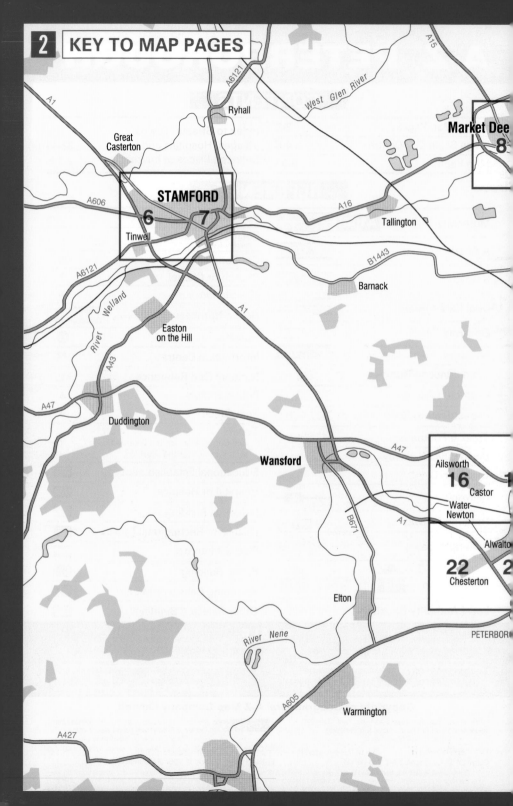

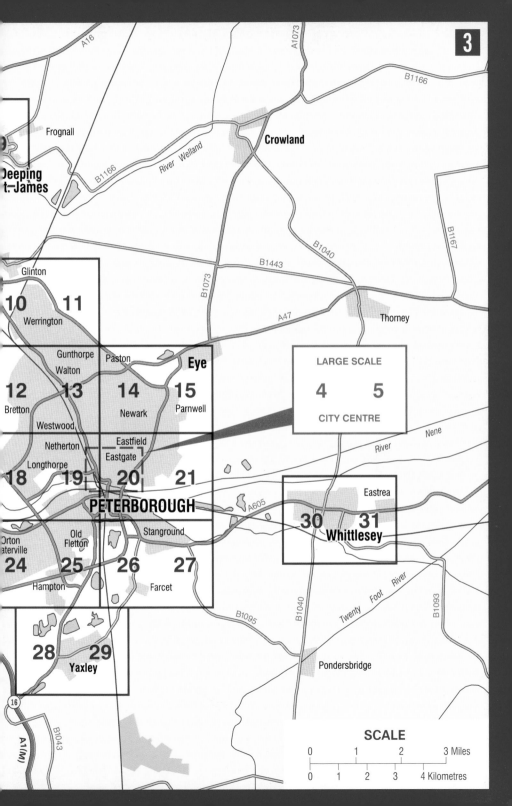

A16

A1073

B1166

Frognall

River Welland

Crowland

B1166

Deeping St. James

B1040

B1167

B1443

B1073

Glinton

B1040

10 **11**

Werrington

A47

Thorney

Gunthorpe

Paston

Eye

Walton

12 **13** **14** **15**

Bretton

Newark

Parnwell

Westwood

LARGE SCALE

4 **5**

CITY CENTRE

Netherton

Eastfield

Nene

Longthorpe

Eastgate

River

18 **19** **20** **21**

A605

Eastrea

PETERBOROUGH

30 **31**

Old

Stanground

Whittlesey

Fletton

Orton Waterville

24 **25** **26** **27**

Hampton

Farcet

B1040

Twenty Foot River

B1093

B1095

28 **29**

Yaxley

Pondersbridge

16

A1(m)

B1043

SCALE

0   1   2   3 Miles

0   1   2   3   4 Kilometres

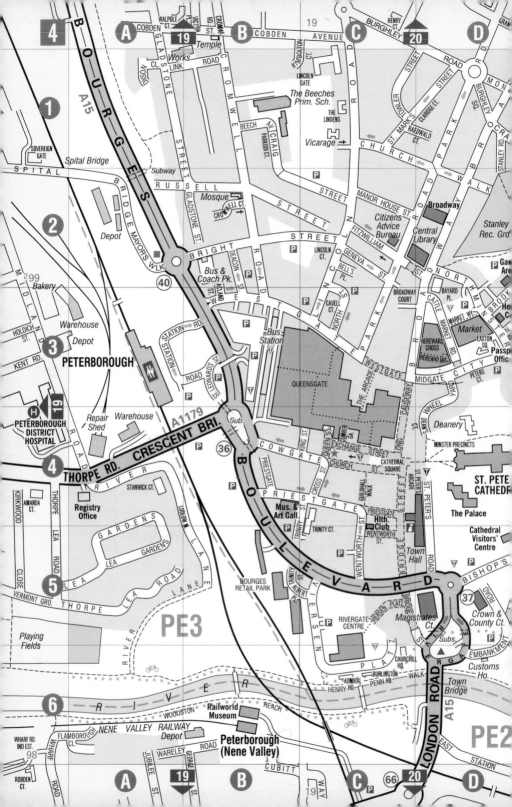

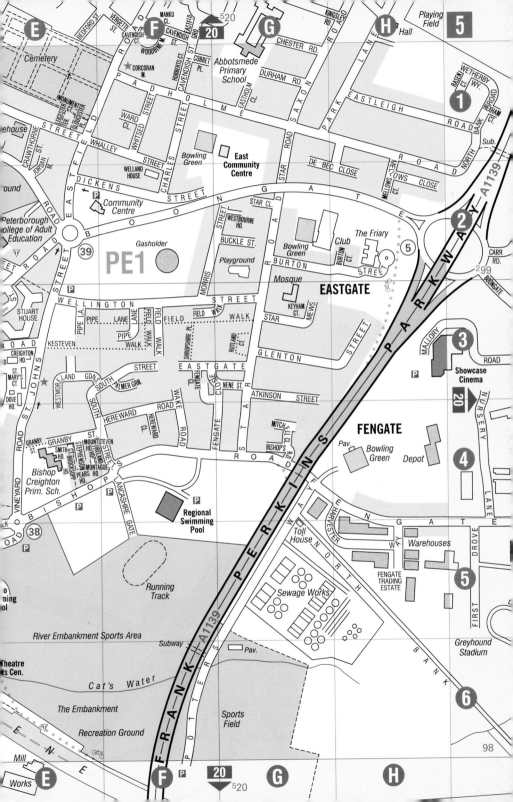

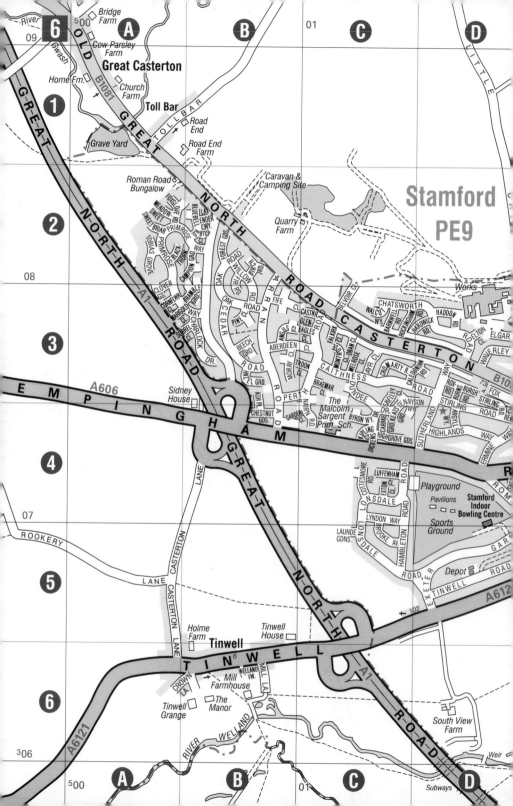

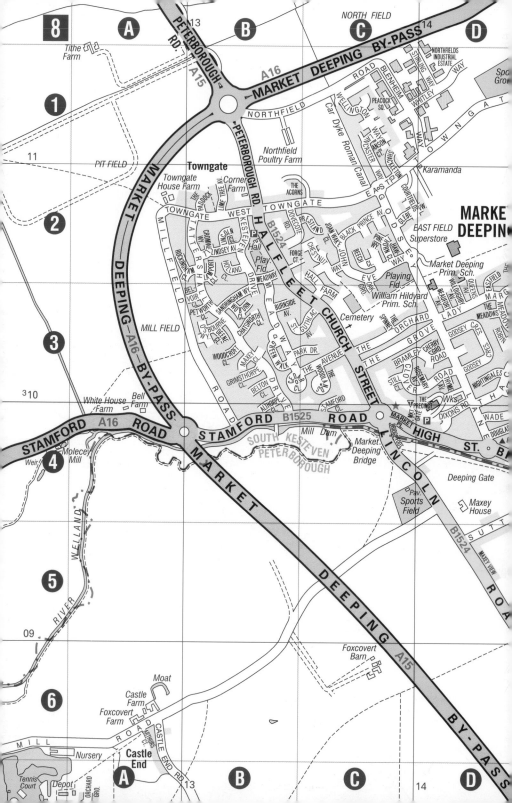

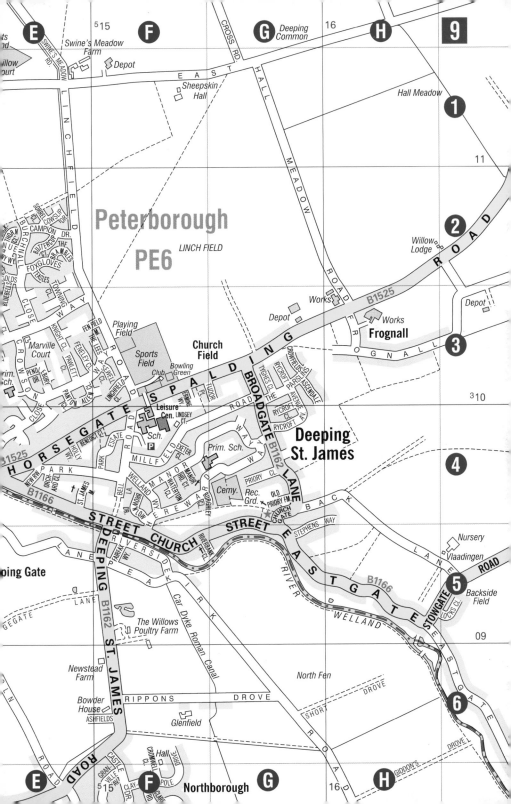

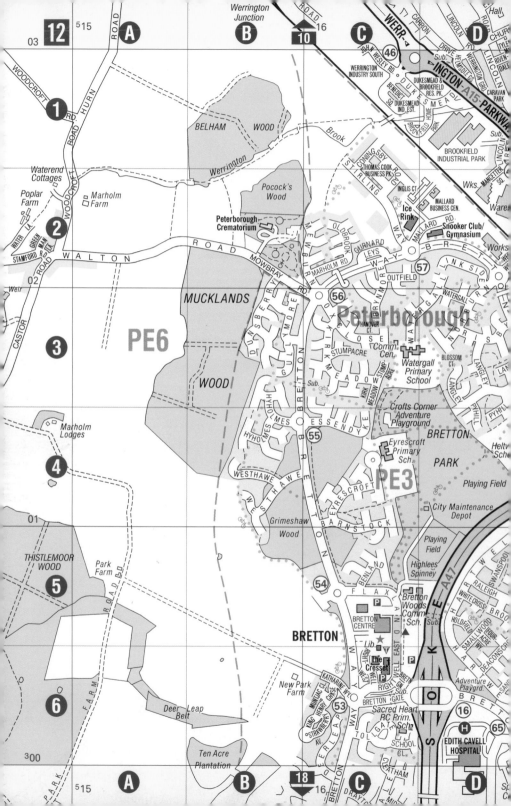

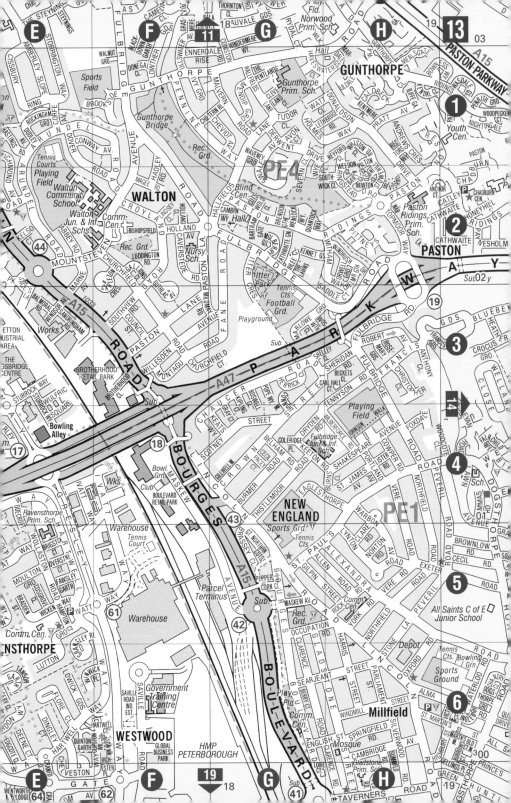

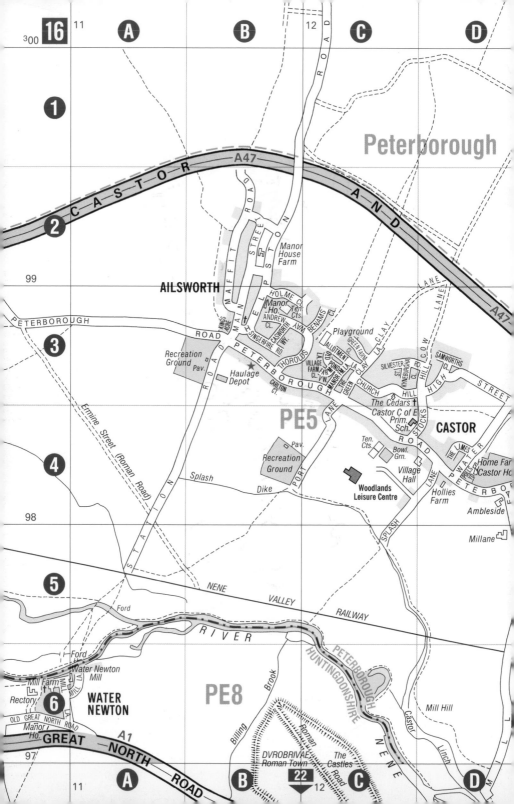

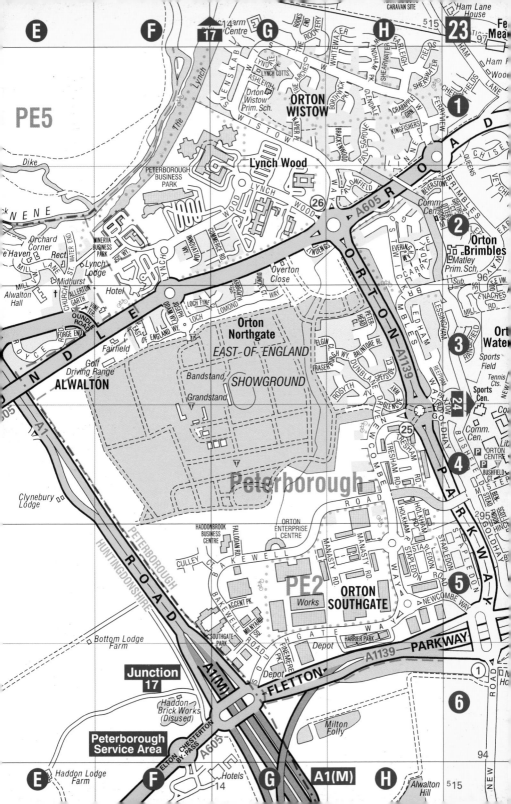

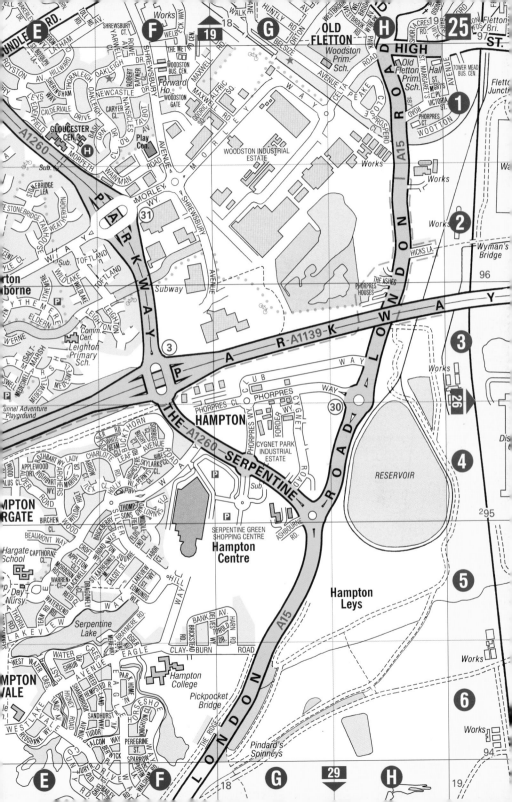

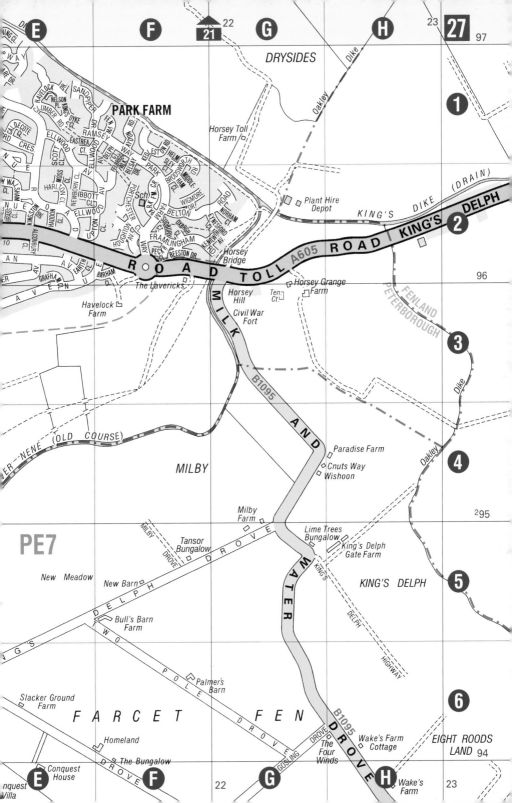

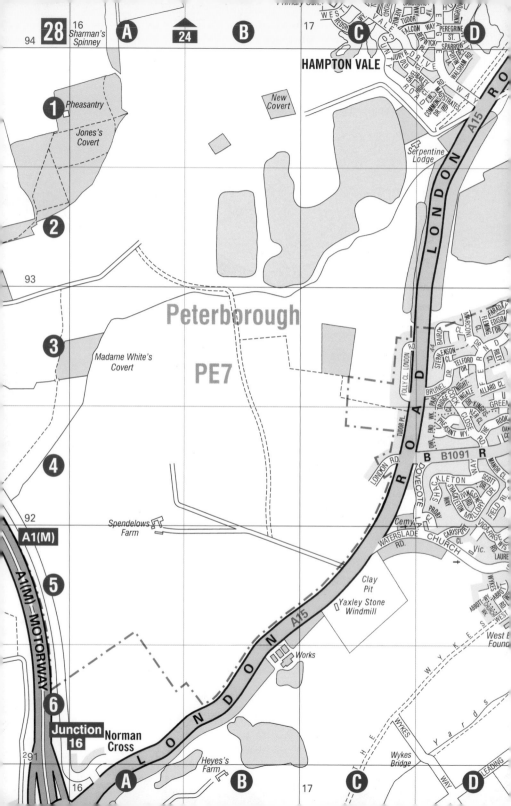

Pheasantry

Jones's Covert

New Covert

HAMPTON VALE

Serpentine Lodge

Peterborough

Madame White's Covert

PE7

93

A1(M)

Spendelows Farm

92

Clay Pit

Yaxley Stone Windmill

Waterslade Rd.

CHURCH

Cemy.

B **B1091** **R**

LONDON ROAD

A15

Works

A1(M) MOTORWAY

Junction 16 Norman Cross

291

West E Found

Wykes Bridge

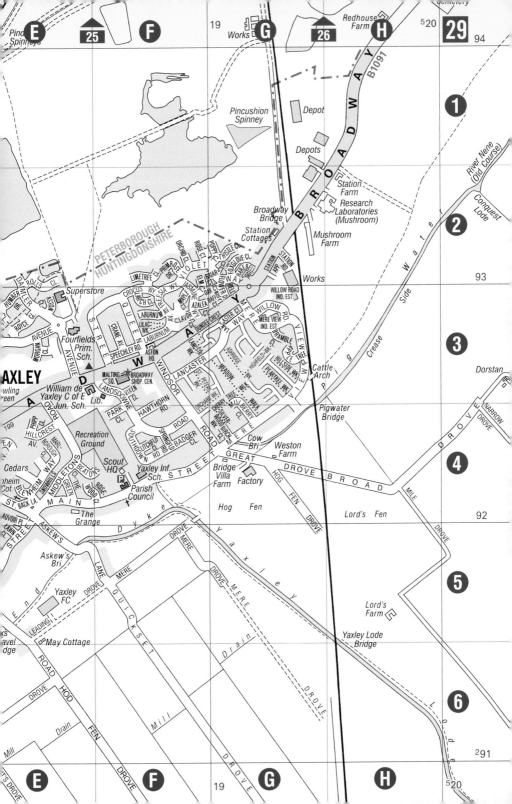

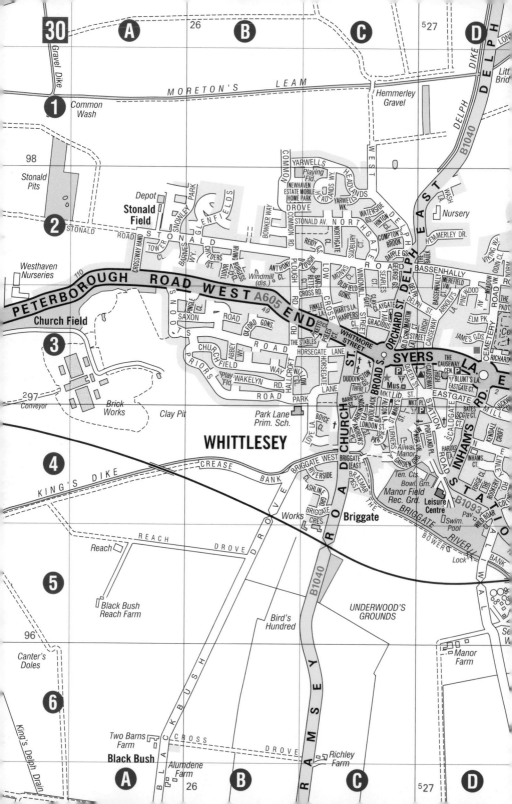

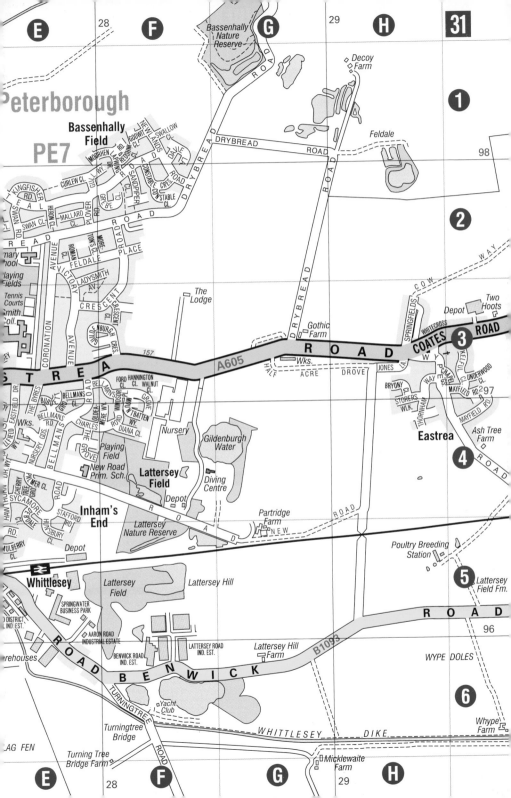

INDEX

Including Streets, Places & Areas, Hospitals & Hospices, Industrial Estates,
Selected Flats & Walkways, Stations and Selected Places of Interest.

HOW TO USE THIS INDEX

1. Each street name is followed by its Postcode District and then by its Locality abbreviation(s) and then by its map reference;
e.g. **Abbotsbury** PE2: Pet . . . .4D **24** is in the PE2 Postcode District and the Peterborough Locality and is to be found in square 4D on page **24**.
The page number is shown in bold type.

2. A strict alphabetical order is followed in which Av., Rd., St., etc. (though abbreviated) are read in full and as part of the street name;
e.g. **Apple Tree Cl.** appears after **Appleton Cl.** but before **Applewood Dr.**

3. Streets and a selection of flats and walkways too small to be shown on the maps, appear in the index with the thoroughfare to which it is connected shown
in brackets; e.g. **Adelaide Gdns.** *PE9: Stam* . . . .**4G 7** *(off Adelaide St.)*

4. Addresses that are in more than one part are referred to as not continuous.

5. Places and areas are shown in the index in **BLUE TYPE** and the map reference is to the actual map square in which the town centre or area is located and
not to the place name shown on the map; e.g. **DOGSTHORPE** **4B 14**

6. An example of a selected place of interest is All Saints Brewery Mus. 4F 7

7. An example of a station is **Peterborough Station (Rail)** . . . .**3H 19 (3A 4)**

8. An example of a hospital or hospice is EDITH CAVELL HOSPITAL 1D 18

9. Map references shown in brackets; e.g. **Acland St.** PE1: Pet . . . .2H **19** (3B **4**) refer to entries that also appear on the large scale pages **4-5**.

GENERAL ABBREVIATIONS

App. : Approach	**Gdns.** : Gardens	**Pk.** : Park
Arc. : Arcade	**Gth.** : Garth	**Pas.** : Passage
Av. : Avenue	**Ga.** : Gate	**Pl.** : Place
Blvd. : Boulevard	**Gt.** : Great	**Res.** : Residential
Bri. : Bridge	**Grn.** : Green	**Ri.** : Rise
Bldgs. : Buildings	**Gro.** : Grove	**Rd.** : Road
Bus. : Business	**Ho.** : House	**Shop.** : Shopping
Cvn. : Caravan	**Ho's.** : Houses	**Sth.** : South
C'way. : Causeway	**Ind.** : Industrial	**Sq.** : Square
Cen. : Centre	**Info.** : Information	**St.** : Street
Cl. : Close	**La.** : Lane	**Ter.** : Terrace
Cotts. : Cottages	**Lit.** : Little	**Trad.** : Trading
Ct. : Court	**Mans.** : Mansions	**Va.** : Vale
Cres. : Crescent	**Mkt.** : Market	**Vw.** : View
Cft. : Croft	**Mdw.** : Meadow	**Vs.** : Villas
Dr. : Drive	**Mdws.** : Meadows	**Vis.** : Visitors
E. : East	**M.** : Mews	**Wlk.** : Walk
Ent. : Enterprise	**Mt.** : Mount	**W.** : West
Est. : Estate	**Mus.** : Museum	**Yd.** : Yard
Fld. : Field	**Nth.** : North	
Flds. : Fields	**Pde.** : Parade	

LOCALITY ABBREVIATIONS

Ail : **Ailsworth**	Gt Cas : **Great Casterton**	Pea : **Peakirk**
Alw : **Alwalton**	Had : **Haddon**	Pet : **Peterborough**
Cas : **Castor**	Hamp : **Hampton**	Pet'f : **Peterfield**
Ches : **Chesterton**	Lit C : **Little Casterton**	Stam : **Stamford**
Deep G : **Deeping Gate**	Mar : **Marholm**	Tin : **Tinwell**
Deep J : **Deeping St James**	Mkt D : **Market Deeping**	Uff : **Uffington**
East : **Eastrea**	Max : **Maxey**	W New : **Water Newton**
Elt : **Elton**	Milk N : **Milking Nook**	W Deep : **West Deeping**
Eye : **Eye**	Newb : **Newborough**	Whit : **Whittlesey**
Far : **Farcet**	Nor X : **Norman Cross**	Wot : **Wothorpe**
Glin : **Glinton**	N'boro : **Northborough**	Yax : **Yaxley**

A

	Addington Way PE4: Pet 6E 11	Allan Av. PE2: Pet 2E 27
	Adelaide Gdns. *PE9: Stam* 4G 7	Allard Cl. PE7: Yax 3D 28
	(off Adelaide St.)	Allen Cl. PE6: Deep J 3E 9
Aaron Rd. Ind. Est. PE7: Whit 5E 31	Adelaide St. PE9: Stam 4G 7	Allen Rd. PE1: Pet 5G 13
Abbey Cl. PE6: Eye 2G 15	Admiral Ho. PE1: Pet 4A 20 (6C 4)	Allerton Gth. PE7: Alw 3E 23
Abbey Rd. PE4: Pet 2E 13	AILSWORTH 3B 16	Allexton Gdns. PE1: Pet 4D 14
Abbey Way PE7: Whit 3B 30	Ainsdale Dr. PE4: Pet 5D 10	Allotment La. PE5: Cas 3C 16
Abbotsbury PE2: Pet 4D 24	Airedale Cl. PE1: Pet 5A 14	All Saints Brewery Mus. 4F 7
Abbott's Cl. PE9: Stam 5H 7	Airedale Rd. PE9: Stam 2E 7	All Saints M. PE9: Stam 4F 7
Abbotts Gro. PE4: Pet 3D 10	Albany Wlk. PE2: Pet 6F 19	All Saints Pl. PE9: Stam 4F 7
Abbott Way PE7: Yax 5D 28	Albert Pl. PE1: Pet 4H 19 (5B 4)	All Saints Rd. PE1: Pet 6A 14
Aberdeen Cl. PE9: Stam 3B 6	Albert Rd. PE9: Stam 4G 7	All Saints St. PE9: Stam 4F 7
Aboyne Av. PE2: Pet 2B 24	Alconbury Cl. PE2: Pet 2E 27	Alma Rd. PE1: Pet 6H 13
Acacia Av. PE1: Pet 3B 14	Aldermans Dr. PE3: Pet 2G 19	Almond Rd. PE1: Pet 4B 14
Accent Pk. PE2: Pet 5G 23	Alder Rd. PE7: Pet 4E 25	Almoners La. PE1: Pet 2G 19
Acer Rd. PE1: Pet 5B 14	Aldsworth Cl. PE1: Pet 5D 14	Alnwick PE2: Pet .4C 24
Acland St. PE1: Pet 2H **19** (3B **4**)	Alexandra Rd. PE1: Pet 5H 13	Althorpe Cl. PE6: Mkt D 4B 8
Acorns, The PE6: Mkt D 2B 8	PE9: Stam 3F 7	Alvis Dr. PE7: Yax 3D 28
Activity & Toddler World 2E 21	Alfreds Way PE4: Pet 5C 10	ALWALTON 3E 23
Adam Ct. PE1: Pet 2E 21	Alfric Sq. PE2: Pet 1G 25	Amanda Ct. PE3: Pet 3G **19** (4A **4**)
Adderley PE3: Pet 4E 13	Aliwal Rd. PE7: Whit 5D 30	Amberley Slope PE4: Pet 6E 11

Ambleside Gdns. PE4: Pet 6G 11
AMF Bowling
  Peterborough 4E 13
Ancaster Rd. PE9: Stam 2E 7
Anchor Ct. PE4: Pet 2H 13
Andrea Cl. PE2: Pet 1C 26
Andrew Cl. PE5: Ail 3B 16
Andrewes Cl. PE7: Far 6B 26
Andrew Rd. PE9: Stam 3F 7
Andrews Cres. PE4: Pet 1H 13
Anglian Cl. PE2: Pet 1D 26
Angus Cl. PE9: Stam 3B 6
Angus Ct. PE3: Pet 2F 19
Anne Rd. PE9: Stam 3E 7
Anson Ct. PE6: Mkt D 1C 8
Anthony Cl. PE1: Pet 3H 13
  PE7: Whit 2B 30
Apex, The PE1: Pet 5A 20
Appleton Cl. PE7: Pet 5E 25
Apple Tree Cl. PE7: Yax 3G 29
Applewood Dr. PE7: Pet 4E 25
Appleyard PE2: Pet 6C 20
Apsley Way PE3: Pet 3C 18
Arbroath Gdns. PE2: Pet 3G 23
Arbury Cl. PE3: Pet 2C 18
Arcade, The PE1: Pet 3A 20 (3C 4)
Archers Wood PE7: Pet 4E 25
Argyll Way PE9: Stam 4D 6
Armley Gro. PE9: Stam 2H 7
Arnold's La. PE7: Whit 3D 30
Arnwood Cen. PE1: Pet 1F 21
Arran Rd. PE9: Stam 3B 6
Arrow Ct. PE7: Pet 4E 25
Arthurs Ct. PE6: Max 6A 8
Artindale PE3: Pet 2C 18
Artis Ct. PE3: Pet 2C 18
Arundel Rd. PE4: Pet 1E 13
Ascendale PE6: Deep J 3G 9
Ascot Dr. PE1: Pet 5B 14
Ashbourne Rd. PE7: Pet 5G 25
Ashburn Cl. PE6: Glin 2B 10
Ash Cl. PE1: Pet 4C 14
Ash Ct. PE1: Pet 4C 14
Ashcroft Gdns. PE1: Pet 6C 14
Ashes, The PE7: Pet 2H 25
Ashfields PE3: Pet 3G 19
  PE6: Deep G 6E 9
Ashleigh PE2: Pet 1G 23
Ashline Gro. PE7: Whit 4C 30
Ash Pk. PE4: Pet 3D 10
Ash Pl. PE9: Stam 3B 6
Ashridge Wlk. PE7: Yax 3G 29
Ash Rd. PE1: Pet 4C 14
Ashton Rd. PE3: Pet 6D 12
Askew's La. PE7: Yax 5E 29
Aster Dr. PE4: Pet 6F 11
Aston Ho. PE7: Yax 3F 29
Astore Pk. PE1: Pet 2E 21
Atherstone Av. PE3: Pet 1D 18
Atkinson St. PE1: Pet 3C 20 (3G 5)
Auborn Gdns. PE3: Pet 2C 18
Aubretia Av. PE4: Pet 6F 11
Audley Ga. PE3: Pet 2D 18
Augusta Cl. PE1: Pet 5E 15
Austin Ct. PE7: Yax 3D 28
Austin Friar's La. PE9: Stam 5F 7
Austin St. PE9: Stam 5F 7
Avenue, The PE6: Mkt D 3C 8
Avon Ct. PE4: Pet 1G 13
Axiom Av. PE3: Pet 1E 19
Axiom Ct. PE9: Stam 5H 7
Aydon Rd. PE2: Pet 1F 27
Ayr Cl. PE9: Stam 3C 6
Ayres Dr. PE2: Pet 1C 26
Azalea Cl. PE3: Pet 3C 18
Azalea Ct. PE7: Yax 3F 29

B

Back La. PE6: Deep J 4G 9
  PE6: Eye 1H 15
  PE7: Yax 4E 29
  PE9: Stam 4G 7
Bacon's Holme La. PE4: Pet 1B 14
Bader Cl. PE3: Pet 5E 13
Badger Cl. PE7: Yax 4F 29
Badington Cl. PE2: Pet 5F 19
Bagley End PE4: Pet 2B 14
Bailey Way PE2: Pet 5F 19
Bain Cl. PE9: Stam 2G 7
Bainton Rd. PE6: Milk N 1H 11

Baird Cl. PE7: Yax 3D 28
Bakers La. PE2: Pet 6G 19
Bakewell Rd. PE2: Pet 5G 23
Bala Ct. PE4: Pet 6G 11
Baldwin Dr. PE2: Pet 5G 19
Balintore Ri. PE2: Pet 3H 23
Balmoral Rd. PE4: Pet 3E 13
Bamber St. PE1: Pet 1H 19
Bank Av. PE7: Pet 5F 25
Bank Cl. PE7: Whit 5D 30
Barber Cl. PE2: Pet 1C 26
Barbers Hill PE4: Pet 2D 10
Bardney PE2: Pet 3C 24
Barford Cl. PE2: Pet 6E 19
Barham Cl. PE2: Pet 2F 27
Barkston Dr. PE1: Pet 5B 14
Barley M. PE2: Pet 6F 19
Barnack Bus. Pk. PE1: Pet 1F 21
Barnack Rd. PE9: Stam 5G 7
Barnards Ct. PE3: Pet 2B 18
Barnard Way PE3: Pet 2B 18
Barnes Way PE4: Pet 1D 12
  PE7: Whit 2A 30
Barn Hill PE9: Stam 4F 7
Barn Hill M. PE9: Stam 4F 7
                      (off Barn Hill)
Barnoak Rd. PE6: Newb 2H 11
Barns Cl. PE4: Pet 6D 10
Barnstock PE3: Pet 4C 12
Barnwell Rd. PE9: Stam 3C 6
Baron Ct. PE4: Pet 5F 11
Barons Way PE7: Whit 5G 7
Barretts Cl. PE7: Whit 2C 30
Barrowfield PE1: Pet 4E 15
Barr's St. PE7: Whit 3C 30
Bartram Ga. PE4: Pet 2G 13
Basil Grn. PE2: Pet 1E 25
Bassenhally Ct. PE7: Whit 3D 30
Bassenhally Nature Reserve 1G 31
Bassenhally Rd. PE7: Whit 2D 30
Bates Ct. PE7: Whit 4D 30
Bath Row PE9: Stam 5F 7
Bathurst PE2: Pet 3C 24
Baulk, The PE7: Whit 2D 30
Bayard Pl. PE1: Pet 3D 4
Bayston Ct. PE2: Pet 5G 19
Beatons Cl. PE7: Yax 4E 29
Beaufort Av. PE6: Mkt D 3D 8
Beaulieu Ct. PE6: Eye 1G 15
Beaumont Way PE7: Pet 5E 25
Beauvale Gdns. PE4: Pet 6G 11
Beauvoir Pl. PE7: Yax 4E 29
Beckets Cl. PE7: Whit 3H 13
Beckingham PE2: Pet 4B 24
Bede Pl. PE1: Pet 5A 14
Bedford St. PE1: Pet 1B 20 (1E 5)
Beech Av. PE1: Pet 2H 19 (1B 4)
Beech Cl. PE6: Mkt D 2C 8
Beech Gro. PE9: Stam 3B 6
Beech La. PE6: Deep J 1G 15
Beech Rd. PE6: Glin 1A 10
Beechwood Cl. PE1: Pet 4C 14
Beeston Dr. PE2: Pet 2F 27
Belgic Sq. PE1: Pet 2E 21
Belgravia Ho. PE1: Pet 3G 19
Belham Rd. PE1: Pet 4G 13
Bellamy Ct. PE2: Pet 1C 26
Bell Cotts. PE9: Stam 4G 7
                   (off St Leonard's St.)
Belle Vue PE2: Pet 1C 26
Bell La. PE6: Deep J 4F 9
Bellmans Cl. PE7: Whit 3E 31
Bellmans Gro. PE7: Whit 3F 31
Bellmans Rd. PE7: Whit 4E 31
Bell's Pl. PE1: Pet 2A 20 (2C 4)
Belsay Dr. PE2: Pet 2F 27
Belsize Av. PE2: Pet 6G 19
Belton Cl. PE6: Mkt D 3B 8
Belton Gdns. PE9: Stam 4G 7
Belton Rd. PE2: Pet 2F 27
Belton St. PE9: Stam 4G 7
Belvoir Cl. PE6: Mkt D 3B 8
  PE9: Stam 3C 6
Belvoir Way PE1: Pet 3C 14
Benams Cl. PE5: Cas 3C 16
Benedict Ct. PE6: Deep J 4E 9
Benedict Sq. PE4: Pet 1C 12
Benland PE3: Pet 5C 12
Benstead PE2: Pet 4A 24

Bentley Av. PE7: Yax 3D 28
Bentley St. PE9: Stam 3G 7
Benwick Rd. PE7: Whit 6F 31
Benwick Rd. Ind. Est. PE7: Whit 6F 31
                         (not continuous)
Benyon Gro. PE2: Pet 3D 24
Berkeley Ct. PE9: Stam 3H 7
Berkeley Rd. PE3: Pet 2E 19
Berrybut Way PE9: Stam 2H 7
Berry Ct. PE1: Pet 6G 13
Berwick Pl. PE7: Pet 6F 25
Bess Wright's Drove PE7: Yax 6E 29
Bettles Cl. PE1: Pet 5A 14
Beverley Gdns. PE9: Stam 3E 7
Beverstone PE2: Pet 2H 23
Bevishall PE4: Pet 2H 13
Bew Cl. PE2: Pet 3D 26
Bickleigh Wlk. PE3: Pet 2C 18
Bifield PE2: Pet 4B 24
Big Sky Play Cen. 1F 25
Birch Cl. PE7: Yax 4G 29
Birchen Cl. PE7: Pet 4E 25
Birch Rd. PE9: Stam 2B 6
Birchtree Av. PE1: Pet 4A 14
Birchwood PE2: Pet 4C 24
Birkdale Av. PE4: Pet 6D 10
Bishops Cl. PE1: Pet 6D 14
Bishopsfield PE4: Pet 2F 13
Bishop's Rd. PE1: Pet 4A 20 (5D 4)
BLACK BUSH 6A 30
Blackbush Drove PE7: Whit 6A 30
Blackdown Gth. PE4: Pet 6F 11
Blackfriars St. PE9: Stam 4G 7
Blackmead PE2: Pet 3D 24
Black Path PE9: Stam 3G 7
                      (off Conduit Rd.)
Black Prince Av. PE6: Mkt D 2C 8
Blackstone's Ct. PE9: Stam 3H 7
                    (off St Georges Av.)
Blackthorn PE9: Stam 2A 6
Blackthorn Cl. PE6: Deep J 2E 9
Blackwell Rd. PE7: Pet 5E 25
Blandford Gdns. PE1: Pet 4E 15
Blashfield Cl. PE9: Stam 3E 7
Blenheim Ct. PE9: Stam 4F 7
Blenheim Way PE6: Mkt D 1C 8
  PE7: Yax 4E 29
Blossom Ct. PE3: Pet 3D 12
Bluebell Av. PE1: Pet 3A 14
Bluebell Rd. PE9: Stam 2B 6
Bluebells PE6: Deep J 4F 9
Bluebell Wlk. PE1: Pet 4A 18
Blunt's La. PE7: Whit 3D 30
Bodesway PE2: Pet 3D 24
Boleyn Av. PE2: Pet 3D 24
Boongate PE1: Pet 2B 20 (2F 5)
Borrowdale Cl. PE4: Pet 6G 11
Borthwick Pk. PE2: Pet 1H 23
Boswell Cl. PE1: Pet 3G 13
Botolph Bri. Ind. Est. PE2: Pet 6F 19
Botolph Grn. PE2: Pet 6E 19
Boulevard Retail Pk. PE1: Pet 4F 13
Bourges Blvd. PE1: Pet 4F 13 (1A 4)
Bourges Retail Pk. PE1: Pet .4H 19 (5B 4)
Bower, The PE7: Whit 4C 30
Bower Cl. PE1: Pet 6C 14
Bowker Way PE7: Whit 2B 30
Bowness Way PE4: Pet 1H 13
Boxgrove Cl. PE6: Eye 1H 15
Boyce Cl. PE7: Whit 4C 30
Bozeat Way PE3: Pet 5E 13
Brackenwood PE2: Pet 1H 23
Brackley Cl. PE3: Pet 2F 19
Bradden St. PE3: Pet 5E 13
Bradegate Dr. PE1: Pet 4E 15
Bradwell Rd. PE3: Pet 3C 18
Braemar Cl. PE9: Stam 3C 6
Braemar Gdns. PE7: Whit 4C 30
Brailsford Cl. PE3: Pet 1C 18
Bramall Ct. PE3: Pet 2D 18
Bramble Cl. PE7: Whit 4D 30
  PE7: Yax 3G 29
Bramble Gro. PE9: Stam 3B 6
Brambles, The PE6: Deep J 2E 9
Bramley Rd. PE6: Mkt D 3C 8
Brampton Ct. PE2: Pet 1D 26
Brancepeth Pl. PE2: Pet 6G 19
Branston Ri. PE1: Pet 4D 14
Brassey Cl. PE1: Pet 5G 13
Braybrook PE2: Pet 4C 24
Braymere Rd. PE7: Pet 5F 25
Brazenose La. PE9: Stam 4G 7

Breamore Gdns. PE3: Pet 2D 18
Brendon Gth. PE4: Pet 2G 13
BRETTON 5C 12
Bretton Cen. PE3: Pet 5C 12
Bretton Ga. PE3: Pet 6C 12
Bretton Grn. PE3: Pet 6C 12
Bretton Ind. Area PE3: Pet 3E 13
Bretton Way PE3: Pet 3B 18
Brewerne PE2: Pet 3E 25
Brewster Av. PE1: Pet 5H 19
Breydon Cen. PE1: Pet 2D 20
Briar Way PE1: Pet 6C 14
Brickberry Cl. PE7: Whit 5E 25
Brickstead Rd. PE7: Pet 5F 25
Bridge Foot PE6: Mkt D 4C 8
Bridgegate La. PE6: Deep G 5E 9
Bridgehill Rd. PE6: Newb 3G 11
Bridge St. PE1: Pet 3A 20 (5C 4)
   PE6: Deep J 4D 8
BRIGGATE 4C 30
Briggate Cres. PE7: Whit 4C 30
Briggate E. PE7: Whit 4C 30
Briggate W. PE7: Whit 4B 30
Bright St. PE1: Pet 2H 19 (2B 4)
Brigstock Ct. PE3: Pet 5E 13
Brimbles Way PE2: Pet 2A 24
Bringhurst PE2: Pet 3C 24
Bristol Av. PE4: Pet 6D 10
Briton Ct. PE2: Pet 6D 20
Broad Cl. PE1: Pet 6D 14
Broad Drove PE7: Yax 4H 29
Broadgate La. PE6: Deep J 3G 9
Broadlands, The PE1: Pet 6E 15
Broad St. PE7: Whit 3C 30
   PE9: Stam .4F 7
Broadway PE1: Pet 3A 20 (3C 4)
   PE7: Yax, Far 4D 28
Broadway Ct. PE1: Pet 3A 20 (3C 4)
Broadway Gdns. PE1: Pet 6B 14
Broadway Shop. Cen. PE7: Yax 3F 29
Broadway Theatre, The & Cinema 2D 4
Brocklesby Gdns. PE3: Pet 2E 19
Brocksopp Ho. PE1: Pet 4E 5
Brodsworth Rd. PE2: Pet 2F 27
Brooke Av. PE9: Stam 5C 6
Brookfield Home Pk. PE4: Pet 1C 12
Brookfield Ind. Pk. PE4: Pet 1D 12
Brookfurlong PE3: Pet 5D 12
Brook La. PE7: Far 5C 26
Brookside PE4: Pet 1F 13
Brook St. PE1: Pet 3A 20 (3D 4)
Broom Cl. PE1: Pet 3A 14
   (not continuous)
Brotherhood Cl. PE4: Pet 3F 13
Brotherhood Retail Pk.
   PE4: Pet .3E 13
Brownlow Dr. PE6: Deep J 4F 9
Brownlow Quay PE9: Stam 4G 7
Brownlow Rd. PE1: Pet 5A 14
Brownlow St. PE9: Stam 4G 7
Brownlow Ter. PE9: Stam 4G 7
   (off Back La.)
Brudenell PE2: Pet 5A 24
Brunel Dr. PE7: Yax 3D 28
Brynmore PE3: Pet 3C 12
Bryony Cl. PE7: East 3H 31
Bryony Way PE6: Deep J 2E 9
Buckland Cl. PE3: Pet 2D 18
Buckles Gdns. PE7: Whit 3E 31
Buckle St. PE1: Pet 2C 20 (2G 5)
Buckminster Pl. PE1: Pet 4D 14
Buckthorn Rd. PE7: Pet 4F 25
Bugle La. PE9: Stam 4F 7
   (off Castle St.)
Bullock Rd. PE7: Had 6A 22
Buntings La. PE7: Far 3B 26
Burchnall Cl. PE6: Deep J 2E 9
Burdett Gro. PE7: Whit 3E 31
Burford Way PE1: Pet 5D 14
Burghley Cl. PE6: Deep J 4F 9
Burghley Ct. PE9: Stam 4G 7
   (off Recreation Ground Rd.)
Burghley La. PE9: Stam 5G 7
Burghley Rd. PE1: Pet 1A 20 (1C 4)
   PE9: Stam .2E 7
Burghley Sq. PE1: Pet 2A 20 (1D 4)
Burlington Ho. PE1: Pet 4A 20 (6C 4)
Burmer Rd. PE1: Pet 4G 13
Burns Cl. PE1: Pet 4H 13
Burnside Av. PE6: Mkt D 3B 8
Burns Rd. PE9: Stam 3D 6
Burrows Ct. PE1: Pet 6A 14

Burswood PE2: Pet 5B 24
Burton Ct. PE1: Pet 2C 20 (2H 5)
Burton St. PE1: Pet 2C 20 (2G 5)
Burwell Reach PE2: Pet 6E 19
Burystead PE2: Pet 5B 20
Bushfield PE2: Pet 4A 24
Bushfield Ct. PE2: Pet 4A 24
Bushfield Sports Cen. 3A 24
Bushy Ct. PE7: Pet 4F 25
Buttercup Cl. PE9: Stam 2B 6
Buttercup Ct. PE6: Deep J 2E 9
Buttermere Pl. PE4: Pet 6G 11
Byres, The PE7: Whit 4E 31
Byron Cl. PE2: Pet 1D 26
Byron Way PE9: Stam 4C 6
Bythorn Rd. PE2: Pet 1C 26
Bythorn Way PE2: Pet 1C 26

C

Caithness Rd. PE9: Stam 3C 6
Calcot St. PE7: Pet 5F 25
Caldbeck Cl. PE4: Pet 1H 13
Caldecote Cl. PE2: Pet 1E 27
Caldervale PE2: Pet 1E 25
Caledonian Rd. PE9: Stam 3C 6
Cambrian Way PE4: Pet 2G 13
Cambridge Av. PE1: Pet 6H 13
Cambridge Rd. PE9: Stam 3E 7
Camelia Cl. PE4: Pet 6F 11
Campaign Av. PE2: Pet 5F 19
Campbell Dr. PE4: Pet 5G 11
Campion Dr. PE6: Deep J 2E 9
Campion Gro. PE9: Stam 2B 6
Campion Rd. PE1: Pet 3B 14
Candidus Ct. PE4: Pet 4D 10
Candy St. PE7: Pet 5G 19
Cane Av. PE2: Pet 5F 19
Canonsfield PE4: Pet 5C 10
Canterbury Rd. PE4: Pet 6D 10
Canwell PE2: Pet 5E 11
Capthorne Cl. PE7: Pet 5E 25
Cardinals Ga. PE4: Pet 5C 10
Carisbrook Ct. PE2: Pet 5C 18
Carisbrooke Gro. PE9: Stam 4C 6
Carleton Cres. PE4: Pet 3F 13
Carl Hall Ct. PE1: Pet 3H 13
Carlton Cl. PE5: Cas 3B 16
Carmel Av. PE2: Pet 5G 19
Carradale PE2: Pet 2H 23
Carrier Cl. PE2: Pet 5F 19
Carron Dr. PE4: Pet 6C 10
Carr Rd. PE1: Pet 2D 20 (2H 5)
Carr Rd. Ind. Est. PE1: Pet 2D 20
Carters Cl. PE3: Pet 2B 18
Cartmel Way PE6: Eye 1G 15
Caryer Cl. PE2: Pet 1F 25
Carysfort Cl. PE7: Yax 5D 28
Casterton La. PE9: Tin 5A 6
Casterton Rd. PE9: Stam 3C 6
   (not continuous)
Castle Dr. PE6: N'boro 6F 9
Castle Dyke PE9: Stam 5F 7
CASTLE END .6A 8
Castle End Rd. PE6: Max 6A 8
Castle La. PE9: Stam 5F 7
   (off St Peter's Va.)
Castle St. PE9: Stam 4F 7
CASTOR 3C 16
Castor and Ailsworth By-Pass
   PE5: Ail, Cas 2A 16
Castor Rd. PE6: Mar 1F 17
Casworth Way PE5: Ail 3B 16
Cathedral Grn. PE1: Pet 2A 20 (1D 4)
Cathedral Sq. PE1: Pet 3A 20 (4C 4)
Catherine Cl. PE2: Pet 6D 18
Cathwaite PE4: Pet 2H 13
Catkins, The PE1: Pet 3C 14
   (off Scalford Dr.)
Catley PE4: Pet 2A 14
Cattle Mkt. Rd. PE1: Pet 3A 20 (3D 4)
Causeway Cen., The PE7: Whit 3D 30
Causeway M. PE7: Whit 3D 30
   (off High Causeway)
Cavell Cl. PE3: Pet 1D 18
Cavell Ct. PE1: Pet 3C 4
Cavendish Ct. PE1: Pet 1F 5
Cavendish St. PE1: Pet 1B 20 (1F 5)
Caverstede Rd. PE4: Pet 2F 13
Cecil Ct. PE9: Stam 4G 7
   (off Wharf Rd.)

Cecil Pacey Ct. PE1: Pet 4G 13
Cecil Rd. PE1: Pet 5A 14
Cedar Cl. PE6: Mkt D 3B 8
Cedar Gro. PE3: Pet 3B 14
Cedar Rd. PE9: Stam 3B 6
Celta Rd. PE2: Pet 1H 29
Celtic Cl. PE2: Pet 6D 20
Cemetery Rd. PE7: Whit 3D 30
Central Av. PE1: Pet 5B 14
Central Sq. PE2: Pet 2D 26
Cerris Rd. PE1: Pet 4B 14
Chadburn PE4: Pet 2A 14
Chadburn Cen. PE4: Pet 2A 14
Chain Cl. PE1: Pet 5B 14
Challenger Way PE1: Pet 6F 15
Chancery La. PE6: Eye 1F 15
Chandlers PE2: Pet 2A 24
Chantry Cl. PE1: Pet 6A 14
Chapel Gdns. PE7: East 3H 31
Chapel La. PE2: Pet 2B 24
   PE4: Pet 6E 11
Chapel St. PE1: Pet 3B 20 (3D 4)
   PE2: Pet 6C 20
   PE7: Yax 4D 28
Chapel Yd. PE9: Stam 4G 7
Charles Cope Rd. PE2: Pet 2B 24
Charles Rd. PE7: Whit 4E 31
   PE9: Stam .2E 7
Charles St. PE1: Pet 2B 20 (2F 5)
Charlock Dr. PE9: Stam 3B 6
Charlton Cl. PE1: Pet 4D 18
Charnwood Cl. PE2: Pet 6A 20
Chartwell Cl. PE2: Pet 5A 20
Chatsfield PE4: Pet 3C 10
Chatsworth Cl. PE6: Mkt D 3B 8
Chatsworth Pl. PE3: Pet 3D 18
Chatsworth Rd. PE9: Stam 3C 6
Chaucer Rd. PE1: Pet 4F 13
Chelmer Gth. PE4: Pet 3H 13
Cheltenham Cl. PE1: Pet 5B 14
Chelveston Way PE3: Pet 1E 19
Cherryfields PE2: Pet 1A 24
Cherry Gro. PE6: Mkt D 3D 8
Cherryholt La. PE9: Stam 4H 7
Cherryholt Rd. PE9: Stam 4H 7
Cherry Orton Rd. PE2: Pet 3B 24
Cherry Tree Gro. PE7: Whit 4E 31
Cherrytree Gro. PE1: Pet 5C 14
Cherry Tree Wlk. PE7: Yax 4G 29
Chester Rd. PE1: Pet 1C 20 (1G 5)
CHESTERTON 4D 17
Chesterton Gro. PE2: Pet 1D 26
Chestnut Av. PE1: Pet 4B 14
Chestnut Cl. PE6: Glin 1A 10
Chestnut Cres. PE7: Whit 4D 30
Chestnut Gdns. PE9: Stam 4B 6
Chestnut Way PE6: Mkt D 2C 8
Cheviot Av. PE4: Pet 1G 13
Cheyne La. PE9: Stam 3D 6
Cheyney Ct. PE2: Pet 3D 24
Childers St. PE7: Whit 2B 30
Chiltern Ri. PE4: Pet 1F 13
Chippenham M. PE2: Pet 5E 19
Chisenhale Cl. PE2: Pet 1A 24
Christopher Cl. PE1: Pet 3H 13
Church Cl. PE9: Stam 5G 7
Church Dr. PE2: Pet 3B 24
CHURCH FIELD
   PE6 . . . . .3F 9
   PE7 . . . . .3A 30
Churchfield Ct. PE4: Pet 3F 13
Churchfield Rd. PE4: Pet 2F 13
Churchfield Way PE7: Whit 3B 30
Church Ga. PE6: Deep J 4G 9
Church Hill PE5: Cas 3C 16
Churchill Cl. PE7: Far 5C 26
Churchill Ho. PE1: Pet 6C 4
Churchill Rd. PE9: Stam 2E 7
Church La. PE2: Pet 6B 20
   (Burystead)
   PE2: Pet 2B 24
   (Cherry Orton Rd.)
   PE2: Pet 6B 20
   (Fletton Av.)
   PE9: Stam .5G 7
Church St. PE1: Pet 3A 20 (4C 4)
   PE2: Pet 6C 20
   PE4: Pet 6D 10
   PE6: Deep J 5F 9
   PE6: Mkt D .3C 8
   PE7: Alw 3E 23
   PE7: Whit .4C 30

Church St. PE7: Yax 5D 28
  PE9: Stam 5G 7
Church Vw. PE2: Pet 1D 24
Church Vw. Cl. PE2: Pet 6B 20
Church Wlk. PE1: Pet 2A 20 (1C 4)
  PE7: Far 5C 26
  PE7: Yax 5D 28
Cissbury Ring PE4: Pet 1E 13
City Rd. PE1: Pet 3A 20 (3D 4)
Clare Cl. PE9: Stam 4E 7
Clarence Rd. PE1: Pet 6G 13
Clarendon Way PE6: Glin 1B 10
Clare Rd. PE1: Pet 5H 13
  PE6: N'boro 6F 9
Claridge Ct. PE1: Pet 1D 4
Clavering Wlk. PE4: Pet 4D 10
Clayburn Rd. PE7: Pet 6F 25
Claygate PE7: Whit 3C 30
Clay La. PE5: Cas .3C 16
Claypole Dr. PE6: N'boro 6F 9
Clayton PE2: Pet .3C 24
                 (not continuous)
Cleatham PE3: Pet .1C 18
Clement Dr. PE2: Pet 5F 19
Cleveland Ct. PE4: Pet 1G 13
Cleve Pl. PE6: Eye .1G 15
Cliff Cres. PE9: Stam 4F 7
Cliff Rd. PE9: Stam 4F 7
Clifton Av. PE1: Pet 2G 19
Clipston Wlk. PE3: Pet 6F 13
Cloisters, The PE6: Eye 2G 15
Close, The PE9: Stam 3H 7
             (off Melbourne Rd.)
  PE9: Wot 6F 7
Clover Gdns. PE9: Stam 3A 6
Clover Rd. PE6: Mkt D 3C 8
Club Way PE7: Pet 3G 25
Clumber Rd. PE2: Pet 1E 27
Coalville Cotts. PE9: Stam 3G 7
              (off Trafalgar Ter.)
Coates Rd. PE7: East 3H 31
Cobbet Pl. PE1: Pet 2B 20 (1F 5)
Cobden Av. PE1: Pet 1H 19 (1B 4)
Cobden St. PE1: Pet 1H 19 (1A 4)
Cock Cl. Rd. PE7: Yax 3D 28
Coleridge Pl. PE1: Pet 4G 13
College Pk. PE1: Pet 6C 14
Collingham PE2: Pet 4B 24
Collins Ct. PE7: Whit 4D 30
Coltsfoot Dr. PE2: Pet 6G 19
Commerce Rd. PE2: Pet 2G 23
Common Drove PE7: Whit 1B 30
Common Rd. PE7: Whit 2B 30
Commons Dr. PE7: Pet 1D 28
Compton's Brook PE7: Whit 2C 30
Conduit Rd. PE9: Stam 3G 7
Coneygree Rd. PE2: Pet 1C 26
Conifers, The PE2: Pet 1B 24
Coningsby Rd. PE3: Pet 1C 12
Coniston Rd. PE4: Pet 1G 13
Connaught M. PE1: Pet 3G 13
Conquest Drove PE7: Far 6D 26
Constable Cl. PE7: Whit 2F 31
Constable Cres. PE7: Whit 2F 31
Constable M. PE9: Stam 4F 7
Conway Av. PE4: Pet 1E 13
Cookson Cl. PE7: Yax 5D 28
Cookson Wlk. PE7: Yax 5E 29
Copeland PE3: Pet .2B 18
Copeland Cen. PE3: Pet 2B 18
Copper Beech Way PE2: Pet 6B 20
Coppingford Cl. PE2: Pet 1D 26
Copsewood PE4: Pet 5E 11
Corcoran M. PE1: Pet 1F 5
Corfe Av. PE4: Pet 1E 13
Cornflower Cl. PE9: Stam 3A 6
Cornistall Bldgs. PE9: Stam 4G 7
Cornwall Rd. PE9: Stam 3F 7
Coronation Av. PE7: Whit 3E 31
Cosgrove Cl. PE3: Pet 5E 13
Cotswold Cl. PE4: Pet 2G 13
Cottesmore Cl. PE3: Pet 1E 19
Cottesmore Rd. PE9: Stam 4C 6
Cotton End PE3: Pet 3F 13
Council St. PE4: Pet 3F 13
County Rd. PE7: Pet 6E 25
Courtfields PE6: Mkt D 2C 8
Court Health & Fitness Club 2D 12
Courtyard, The PE4: Pet 6E 11
              (off Green, The)
  PE6: Deep J 4D 8
  PE9: Stam 3E 7

Coventry Cl. PE4: Pet 6D 10
Coverdale Wlk. PE4: Pet 4C 10
              (not continuous)
Covert, The PE3: Pet 4D 18
Cowgate PE1: Pet 3H 19 (4B 4)
Cow La. PE5: Cas .3D 16
Cowper Rd. PE1: Pet 4H 13
Cowslip Dr. PE6: Deep J 2E 9
Cow Way PE7: East 3H 31
Crabapple Grn. PE2: Pet 1H 23
Crabtree PE4: Pet .2B 14
Craig St. PE1: Pet 2H 19 (1B 4)
Crane Av. PE7: Yax 3F 29
Cranemore PE4: Pet 5C 10
Cranford Dr. PE3: Pet 1E 19
Crawthorne Rd. PE1: Pet 2A 20 (1D 4)
Crawthorne St. PE1: Pet 2B 20 (1E 5)
Crease Bank PE7: Whit 4B 30
Creighton Ho. PE1: Pet 3E 5
Crescent, The PE2: Pet 6G 19
               (Orton Av.)
  PE2: Pet 2E 25
              (Village, The)
  PE6: Eye 1H 15
Crescent Bri. PE1: Pet 3H 19 (4A 4)
  PE3: Pet 3H 19 (4A 4)
Crescent Cl. PE7: Whit 3F 31
Crescent Rd. PE7: Whit 3E 31
Cresset, The 6C 12
Crester Dr. PE4: Pet 6E 11
Cripple Sidings La. PE1: Pet 5A 20
Crocus Gro. PE1: Pet 3A 14
Crocus Way PE7: Yax 3F 29
Croft, The PE9: Stam 4H 7
             (off Cherryholt Rd.)
Croft Way PE7: Pet 5E 25
Cromarty Rd. PE9: Stam 3C 6
Cromwell Cl. PE6: N'boro 6F 9
Cromwell Ct. PE1: Pet 2H 19 (2B 4)
Cromwell Rd. PE1: Pet 1H 19 (1B 4)
              (not continuous)
Cromwell Way PE6: Mkt D 2B 8
Cropston Rd. PE1: Pet 4E 15
Cross Drove PE7: Whit 6B 30
Cross Keys La. PE9: Stam 4F 7
Cross Rd. PE6: Mkt D 1G 9
  PE7: Whit 3C 30
Cross St. PE1: Pet 3A 20 (4C 4)
  PE7: Far 5D 26
Crossway Hand PE7: Whit 2A 30
Crowfields PE6: Deep J 3G 9
Crowhurst PE4: Pet 4E 11
Crowland Rd. PE6: Eye 1H 15
Crown La. PE9: Tin .6B 6
Crown St. PE1: Pet 4G 13
  PE9: Stam 4F 7
             (off Red Lion St.)
Crowson Way PE6: Deep J 3E 9
Croyland Rd. PE4: Pet 2F 13
Crystal Dr. PE2: Pet 5F 19
Cubitt Way PE2: Pet 5H 19 (6B 4)
Culley Ct. PE2: Pet .5F 23
Cumber Ga. PE1: Pet 3A 20 (4C 4)
Cumberland Ho. PE1: Pet 3E 5
Cunningham Rd. PE2: Pet 5G 19
Curlew Cl. PE7: Whit 2E 31
Curlew Gro. PE2: Pet 6D 20
Curlew Wlk. PE6: Deep J 3D 8
Cygnet Pk. Ind. Est. PE7: Pet 4G 25
Cygnet Rd. PE7: Pet 4G 25
Cypress Cl. PE3: Pet 3C 18

D

Daffodil Gro. PE2: Pet 6C 20
Daimler Av. PE7: Yax 3E 29
Dalby Ct. PE1: Pet 3C 14
Dale Cl. PE2: Pet 2B 24
Danegeld Pl. PE9: Stam 4G 7
Danes Cl. PE1: Pet .1C 20
Daniel Ct. PE9: Stam 5G 7
Danish Ct. PE4: Pet 5C 10
Dapple Gdns. PE7: Whit 2C 30
Darwin Cl. PE9: Stam 2E 7
David Chalmers Cl. PE1: Pet 5H 19
David's Cl. PE4: Pet 5B 10
David's La. PE4: Pet 5C 10
Davie La. PE7: Whit 1F 31
Daymond St. PE2: Pet 5F 19
Deaconscroft PE3: Pet 6D 12
Deacon St. PE1: Pet 2H 19 (2B 4)

Dean's Ct. PE1: Pet 3A 20 (4D 4)
Debdale PE2: Pet 3A 24
Debdale Ct. PE7: Whit 4E 31
De Bec Cl. PE1: Pet 2C 20 (2G 5)
Deene Cl. PE6: Mkt D 3B 8
Deene Ct. PE2: Pet .6E 13
DEEPING GATE 5E 9
DEEPING ST JAMES 4G 9
Deeping St James Rd.
  PE6: Deep G, N'boro 5F 9
Deepings Leisure Cen. 4F 9
Deerhurst Way PE6: Eye 1H 15
Deerleap PE3: Pet .6C 12
Deer Valley Rd. PE2: Pet 5G 19
Delamere Cl. PE1: Pet 6C 14
Delapre Ct. PE6: Eye 1G 15
Dell, The PE2: Pet .6G 19
Delph PE7: Whit 2C 30
Delph Sq. PE2: Pet .1F 27
Delph St. PE7: Whit 3C 30
Delves Way PE7: Pet 5F 25
Demontford Ct. PE2: Pet 5H 19
Denham Wlk. PE3: Pet 1E 19
Denis Dr. PE2: Pet .3C 24
Denmark Dr. PE2: Pet 3C 24
Denton Rd. PE2: Pet 1D 26
Derby Dr. PE1: Pet .5C 14
Derwent Dr. PE4: Pet 1G 13
Derwood Gro. PE4: Pet 4D 10
Desborough Av. PE2: Pet 3D 26
Diana Cl. PE7: Whit 4F 31
Dickens Dr. PE9: Stam 4C 6
Dickens St. PE1: Pet 2B 20 (2E 5)
Dingley Ct. PE3: Pet 6E 13
Dixons Rd. PE6: Mkt D 4D 8
Doddington Dr. PE3: Pet 3D 18
Dodson Way PE1: Pet 3F 21
DOGSTHORPE 4B 14
Dogsthorpe Gro. PE1: Pet 6A 14
Dogsthorpe Rd. PE1: Pet 4A 14
              (not continuous)
Donaldson Dr. PE4: Pet 1H 13
Donegal Cl. PE4: Pet 1F 13
Dorchester Cres. PE1: Pet 4D 14
Doughty St. PE9: Stam 2H 7
Douglas Rd. PE6: Mkt D 4D 8
Dovecote Cl. PE1: Pet 4A 14
Dovecote La. PE7: Yax 4D 28
Dovecote Rd. PE6: Mkt D 2B 8
Dove Ho. PE1: Pet 3E 5
Dover Rd. PE4: Pet 1E 13
Down Ga. PE3: Pet 4B 18
Downing Cres. PE9: Stam 2F 7
Dragonfly Cl. PE7: Pet 5E 25
Drain Rd. PE6: Newb 3H 11
Drayton PE3: Pet 1C 18
Driffield Way PE2: Pet 5F 19
Drift Av. PE9: Stam .3G 7
Drift Gdns. PE9: Stam 2H 7
Drift Rd. PE9: Stam .3G 7
Droveway, The PE6: Pet 2H 21
Drybread Rd. PE7: East 3G 31
  PE7: Whit 2E 31
Dryden Rd. PE1: Pet 4G 13
Dry Leys PE2: Pet 1E 25
Duckworth Cl. PE7: Whit 3D 30
Duddington Gdns. PE7: Whit 3C 30
Dudley Av. PE2: Pet .3E 5
Dukesmead PE4: Pet 1C 12
Dukesmead & Brookfield Res. Pk.
  PE4: Pet 1C 12
Dukesmead Ind. Est. PE4: Pet 1C 12
Duke St. PE2: Pet .6A 20
Dunblane Dr. PE2: Pet 3H 23
Duncombes Yd. PE9: Stam 5G 7
Dundee Ct. PE2: Pet 2G 23
Dundee Crest PE7: Yax 3F 29
Dundee Dr. PE9: Stam 3C 6
Dunsberry PE3: Pet .3B 12
Dunstan Ct. PE1: Pet 6C 14
Durham Rd. PE1: Pet 2C 20 (1G 5)
Dyson Cl. PE1: Pet 2H 19 (1A 4)

E

Eaglesthorpe PE1: Pet 4G 13
Eagle Way PE7: Pet 6F 25
Eames Gdns. PE1: Pet 5E 15
Earith Cl. PE2: Pet .2E 27
Earls Cl. PE1: Pet 1B 26
Earl Spencer Ct. PE1: Pet 5G 19
Earlswood PE2: Pet 2A 24

Easby Ri. PE6: Pet 1H **15**
East Delph PE7: Whit 2D **30**
Eastern Av. PE1: Pet 3B **14**
Eastern Cl. PE1: Pet 4D **14**
EASTFIELD 1C **20**
Eastfield PE6: Mkt D 2D **8**
Eastfield Dr. PE7: Whit 4E **31**
Eastfield Gro. PE1: Pet 1B **20** (1F **5**)
Eastfield Rd. PE1: Pet 2B **20** (2E **5**)
EASTGATE 2C **20** (3G **5**)
Eastgate PE1: Pet 3B **20** (3F **5**)
  PE6: Deep J 5G **9**
  PE7: Whit 3D **30**
Eastgate Ct. PE7: Whit 3D **30**
Eastgate M. *PE7: Whit* *3D **30***
  (off Eastgate)
Eastholm Cl. PE1: Pet 2C **20** (1G **5**)
Eastleigh Rd. PE1: Pet 2C **20** (1H **5**)
East of England Showground 3G **23**
East of England Way PE2: Pet 3F **23**
EASTREA 3H **31**
Eastrea Ct. PE2: Pet 1E **27**
Eastrea Rd. PE7: Whit, East 3D **30**
E. Station Rd. PE1: Pet 4A **20** (6D **4**)
East St. PE9: Stam 4G **7**
E. Water Cres. PE7: Pet 6E **25**
Eathwaite Grn. PE4: Pet 2G **13**
Edenfield PE2: Pet 1E **25**
Edgcote Cl. PE3: Pet 6E **13**
Edgerley Bus. Pk. PE1: Pet 6F **15**
Edgerley Drain Rd. PE1: Pet 6F **15**
Edgerley Drove PE6: Eye 2F **15**
Edinburgh Av. PE4: Pet 6D **10**
Edinburgh Rd. PE9: Stam 3E **7**
Edis Ct. PE2: Pet 1B **26**
Edison Dr. PE7: Yax 3D **28**
EDITH CAVELL HOSPITAL 1D **18**
Edmonds Cl. PE9: Stam 3H **7**
Edwalton Av. PE1: Pet 2G **19**
Edward Rd. PE9: Stam 2F **7**
Egar Way PE3: Pet 3B **18**
Eight Acres PE9: Stam 4E **7**
Eldern PE2: Pet 3E **25**
Eleanor Cl. PE9: Stam 3E **7**
Elgar Way PE9: Stam 3D **6**
Elizabeth Ct. PE1: Pet 6A **14**
Elizabeth Rd. PE9: Stam 3E **7**
Ellindon PE3: Pet 4E **13**
Elliot Av. PE3: Pet 3B **18**
Ellwood Av. PE2: Pet 1E **27**
Elm Cl. PE6: Mkt D 3D **8**
  PE7: Yax 2F **29**
Elm Cres. PE6: Glin 1A **10**
Elmfield Rd. PE1: Pet 4A **14**
Elmore Rd. PE3: Pet 2C **18**
Elm Pk. PE7: Whit 3D **30**
Elm St. PE2: Pet 6H **19**
  PE9: Stam 4G **7**
Elstone PE2: Pet 3C **24**
Elter Wlk. PE4: Pet 6G **11**
Elton Chesterton By-Pass PE7: Ches 6F **23**
Elton Cl. PE9: Stam 3D **6**
Ely Cl. PE4: Pet 6D **10**
Embankment Rd. PE1: Pet 4A **20** (6D **4**)
Emlyns Gdns. PE9: Stam 3G **7**
Emlyns St. PE9: Stam 3G **7**
Emmanuel Rd. PE9: Stam 2F **7**
Empingham Rd. PE: Tin, Stam 3A **6**
Empson Rd. PE1: Pet 6F **15**
Enfield Gdns. PE3: Pet 1E **19**
  (not continuous)
Engaine PE2: Pet 2D **24**
English St. PE1: Pet 6G **13**
Ennerdale Ri. PE4: Pet 1F **13**
Enterprise Way PE3: Pet 3D **12**
Ermine Cl. PE9: Stam 4D **6**
Ermine Way PE6: Deep J 3F **9**
  PE9: Stam 4D **6**
Eskdale Cl. PE4: Pet 6G **11**
Essendyke PE3: Pet 4C **12**
Essex Rd. PE9: Stam 3E **7**
Everdon Way PE3: Pet 6E **13**
Everingham PE2: Pet 2H **23**
Evesham Way PE6: Eye 1A **10**
Exchange St. PE1: Pet 3A **20** (4C **4**)
Exeter Cl. PE6: Deep J 4F **9**
Exeter Ct. PE9: Stam 4F **7**
Exeter Gdns. PE9: Stam 5D **6**
Exeter Rd. PE1: Pet 5H **13**
Exton Cl. PE9: Stam 4C **6**
EYE 1H **15**
Eyebrook Gdns. PE4: Pet 6G **11**

Eyebury Rd. PE6: Eye 1H **15**
Eye By-Pass PE6: Eye 1F **15**
  PE6: Pet 2C **14**
Eye Rd. PE1: Pet 5E **15**
Eynesford Cl. PE2: Pet 2G **27**
Eyrescroft PE3: Pet 4C **12**

F

Fairchild Way PE1: Pet 4A **14**
Fairfax Way PE6: Deep G 5F **9**
Fairfield Rd. PE2: Pet 5A **20**
Fairmead Way PE3: Pet 3G **19**
Fairweather Ct. PE1: Pet 2E **21**
Falcon La. PE7: Whit 3C **30**
Falcon Way PE7: Pet 6E **25**
Falkirk Cl. PE9: Stam 3C **6**
Fallodan Rd. PE9: Stam 5G **23**
Fallowfield PE2: Pet 2H **23**
Fane Cl. PE9: Stam 2F **7**
Fane Rd. PE4: Pet 3G **13**
Faraday Cl. PE7: Yax 3D **28**
FARCET 5C **26**
Farleigh Flds. PE2: Pet 6H **17**
Farm Vw. PE5: Cas 3C **16**
Farnsworth Ct. PE2: Pet 1B **26**
Far Pasture PE4: Pet 4D **10**
Farriers Ct. PE2: Pet 6F **19**
Farringdon Cl. PE1: Pet 5D **14**
Farthingstones PE6: Glin 1A **10**
Fawsley Gth. PE3: Pet 5E **13**
Fefield M. PE6: Deep J 3E **9**
Felbrigg Wlk. PE2: Pet 1F **27**
Feldale Pl. PE7: Whit 2E **31**
Fellowes Gdns. PE2: Pet 6A **20**
Fellowes Rd. PE2: Pet 6A **20**
Fenbridge Rd. PE4: Pet 5E **11**
Feneley Cl. PE6: Deep J 3E **9**
FENGATE 3D **20** (4H **5**)
Fengate PE1: Pet 3C **20** (4G **5**)
Fengate Cvn. Pk. PE1: Pet 4E **21**
Fengate Cl. PE1: Pet 3C **20** (4G **5**)
  (not continuous)
Fengate Trad. Est. PE1: Pet 4C **20** (5H **5**)
Fenlake Bus. Cen. PE1: Pet 3E **21**
Fenland Cl. *PE7: Whit* *3C **30***
  (off West End)
Fenland District Council Ind. Est.
  PE7: Whit 5E **31**
Fenmere Wlk. PE7: Pet 5F **25**
Fen Vw. PE2: Pet 1F **27**
Ferndale PE7: Yax 3D **28**
Ferndale Way PE1: Pet 2B **14**
Ferry Dr. PE6: Mar 3G **17**
Ferry Mdws. Cvn. Site PE2: Pet 6H **17**
  (not continuous)
Ferry Meadows Country Pk. Vis. Cen. 6H **17**
Ferry Meadows Station
  Nene Valley Railway 6A **18**
Ferryview PE2: Pet 1H **23**
Ferry Rd. PE2: Pet 6D **12**
Ferry Wlk. PE2: Pet 4H **17**
Festival Ct. PE3: Pet 6D **12**
Fieldfare Dr. PE2: Pet 1E **27**
Field Ri. PE7: Yax 4D **28**
Fields End Cl. PE7: Pet 5F **25**
Field Ter. PE7: Far 5C **26**
Field Wlk. PE1: Pet 3B **20** (3F **5**)
  (not continuous)
Fife Cl. PE9: Stam 3B **6**
Figtree Wlk. PE1: Pet 4A **14**
Finchfield PE1: Pet 4E **15**
Finchley Grn. PE1: Pet 1G **19**
Finemere Pk. PE2: Pet 6G **23**
Finkle La. PE7: Whit 3C **30**
Fir Rd. PE9: Stam 2B **6**
First Drift PE9: Wot 1H **9**
First Drove PE1: Pet 4D **20** (5H **5**)
Fitness First Health Club 1G **19**
Fitness Zone 4C **4**
FITZWILLIAM CAPIO HOSPITAL 3A **18**
Fitzwilliam Rd. PE9: Stam 2E **7**
Fitzwilliam St. PE1: Pet 2A **20** (2C **4**)
Five Arches PE2: Pet 1G **23**
Flag Bus. Exchange PE1: Pet 2E **21**
Flag Fen Rd. PE1: Pet 1C **20**
Flag Fen Vis. Cen. 3G **21**
Flamborough Cl. PE2: Pet 4G **19** (6A **4**)
Flaxland PE3: Pet 5C **12**
Flaxley Rd. PE2: Pet 3B **26**
Fleet Drove PE2: Pet 1B **26**
Fleet Way PE2: Pet 1B **26**

Fleming Cl. PE7: Yax 3D **28**
Flemming Ct. PE2: Pet 5F **19**
Fletton Av. PE2: Pet 5A **20**
Fletton Flds. PE2: Pet 6A **20**
Fletton Parkway PE2: Pet 6G **23**
Flore Cl. PE3: Pet 6E **13**
Florence Cl. PE7: Whit 4E **31**
Florence Way PE6: Mkt D 3D **8**
Folly Cl. PE7: Yax 3C **28**
Fontwell Gdns. PE9: Stam 4F **7**
Ford Cl. PE7: Whit 3F **31**
Forder Way PE7: Pet 4G **25**
Forest Gdns. PE9: Stam 2B **6**
Forge Cl. PE7: Whit 4D **30**
Forge Ct. PE6: Mkt D 2B **8**
Forge End PE7: Alw 3E **23**
Forty Acre Rd. PE1: Pet 3D **20**
Foster Rd. PE2: Pet 5F **19**
Foundry Ct. *PE9: Stam* *4E **7***
  (off Foundry Rd.)
Foundry Rd. PE9: Stam 4E **7**
Fountains Pl. PE6: Eye 1H **15**
Four Chimneys Cres. PE7: Pet 5E **25**
Fourth Drove PE1: Pet 2F **21**
Foxcovert Rd. PE4: Pet 2C **10**
  PE6: Pet 1C **10**
Foxcovert Wlk. PE4: Pet 3D **10**
Fox Dale PE9: Stam 3D **6**
Foxdale PE1: Pet 4H **13**
Foxglove Rd. PE9: Stam 2A **6**
Foxgloves PE6: Deep J 2E **9**
Foxley Cl. PE4: Pet 5E **11**
Framlingham Rd. PE2: Pet 2F **27**
Francis Gdns. PE1: Pet 3H **13**
Franklyn Cres. PE1: Pet 5E **15**
Frank Perkins Parkway PE1: Pet 6B **20** (6F **5**)
  PE2: Pet 5B **20**
Fraserburgh Way PE2: Pet 3G **23**
Fraser Cl. PE6: Deep J 3E **9**
Freesia Way PE7: Yax 3F **29**
Freston PE4: Pet 1H **13**
FROGNALL 3H **9**
Frognall PE6: Deep J 3H **9**
Fryers Callis *PE9: Stam* *5G **7***
  (off Wothorpe Rd.)
Fulbridge Rd. PE1: Pet 3H **13**
  PE4: Pet 4E **11**
Fulham Rd. PE3: Pet 1G **19**
Furze Ride PE1: Pet 3B **14**

G

Gainsborough Rd. PE9: Stam 2D **6**
Gala Bingo Club 1G **19**
Gallions Cl. PE4: Pet 2F **13**
Gannocks, The PE2: Pet 2B **24**
Gannocks Cl. PE2: Pet 2B **24**
Garden Cl. PE9: Stam 4B **6**
Garden Gro. PE7: Whit 4C **30**
Garratt Rd. PE9: Stam 5F **7**
Garrick Wlk. PE2: Pet 6B **20**
Garton End Rd. PE1: Pet 5A **14**
Garton St. PE1: Pet 6A **14**
Gascoigne PE4: Pet 4B **10**
Gas La. PE9: Stam 4G **7**
Gas St. PE9: Stam 4G **7**
Gatenby PE4: Pet 5E **11**
Gavel St. PE7: Pet 1C **28**
Gayton Ct. PE3: Pet 6E **13**
Gazeley Gdns. PE7: Far 5B **26**
Geddington Rd. PE2: Pet 5G **19**
Geneva St. PE1: Pet 2A **20** (2C **4**)
George St. PE2: Pet 5H **19** (6B **4**)
Georgian Cl. PE3: Pet 4G **19**
Giddings Cl. PE2: Pet 3B **24**
Giddon's Drove PE6: N'boro 6H **9**
Gildale PE4: Pet 5F **11**
Gildenburgh Av. PE1: Pet 6D **14**
Gillwell M. PE1: Pet 4G **13**
Gilmorton Dr. PE1: Pet 4D **14**
Gilpin St. PE1: Pet 5G **13**
Gipsy La. PE9: Stam 2H **7**
Girton Way PE9: Stam 2E **7**
Gladstone St. PE1: Pet 6G **13** (1A **4**)
Glamis Gdns. PE1: Pet 3D **18**
Glastonbury Cl. PE6: Eye 1G **15**
Glatton Dr. PE2: Pet 1D **26**
Glebe Av. PE2: Pet 3A **24**
Glebe Ct. PE2: Pet 5B **20**
Glebe Rd. PE1: Pet 5A **20**
Glebe Vw. PE6: Mkt D 2C **8**

Glemsford Ri.—Huntsmans Ga.

Glemsford Ri. PE2: Pet 6E **19**
Glen, The PE2: Pet 6B **20**
Glencoe Way PE2: Pet 4H **23**
Glen Cres. PE9: Stam 2G **7**
Glendale PE2: Pet 1H **23**
Gleneagles PE2: Pet 1B **24**
Gleneagles Cl. PE9: Stam 3C **6**
Glenfields PE7: Whit 2B **30**
Glenton St. PE1: Pet 3C **20** (3G **5**)
GLINTON **1B 10**
Glinton By-Pass PE4: Milk N, Pea 2A **10**
PE6: Glin 2A **10**
Glinton Rd. PE6: Milk N 1G **11**
Global Bus. Pk. PE3: Pet 6F **13**
Global Cen. Ind. Est. PE1: Pet 1E **21**
GLOUCESTER CENTRE **1E 25**
Gloucester Pl. PE1: Pet 1E **5**
Gloucester Rd. PE2: Pet 6B **20**
PE9: Stam 3F **7**
Godric Sq. PE2: Pet 1F **25**
Godsey Cres. PE6: Mkt D 3D **8**
Godsey La. PE6: Mkt D 2C **8**
Godwit Cl. PE7: Whit 1F **31**
Goffsmill PE3: Pet 1C **18**
Goldcrest Ct. PE1: Pet 3C **14**
Goldhay Way PE2: Pet 4A **24**
Goldie La. PE2: Pet 1B **24**
Goldsmiths La. PE9: Stam 4G **7**
Gooch's Ct. *PE9: Stam* *4F* **7**
(off Castle St.)
Goodacre PE2: Pet 3C **24**
Goodmans Bus. Pk. PE1: Pet 3E **21**
Goodwin Wlk. PE4: Pet 4D **10**
Goodwood Rd. PE3: Pet 2B **18**
Gordon Av. PE2: Pet 6G **19**
Gordon Way PE2: Pet 6E **19**
Gorse Grn. PE1: Pet 3B **14**
(not continuous)
Gosling Drove PE7: Far 6G **27**
Gostwick PE2: Pet 2H **23**
Gracechurch Ct. PE1: Pet 6C **14**
Gracious St. PE7: Whit 3C **30**
Grafham Cl. PE2: Pet 2E **27**
Grafton Av. PE3: Pet 2E **19**
Granby St. PE1: Pet 3B **20** (4E **5**)
Grange Av. PE1: Pet 5A **14**
Grange Cres. PE2: Pet 2C **24**
Grange Rd. PE3: Pet 2F **19**
Gransley Ri. PE3: Pet 6E **13**
Granville Av. PE6: N'boro 6F **9**
Granville St. PE1: Pet 1A **20** (1D **4**)
Grasmere Gdns. PE4: Pet 6F **11**
Gravel Wlk. PE1: Pet 4A **20** (5D **4**)
Gray Ct. PE1: Pet 4G **13**
GREAT CASTERTON **1A 6**
Great Drove PE7: Yax 4G **29**
Gt. Northern Cotts. PE1: Pet 5G **13**
Great North Rd. PE7: Ches 2D **22**
PE8: W New, Ches 6A **16**
PE9: Tin 1A **6**
Grebe Cl. PE7: Whit 2F **31**
Green, The PE4: Pet 6E **11**
PE5: Cas 3C **16**
PE6: Glin 1A **10**
PE7: Yax 4E **29**
Greenacres PE4: Pet 5C **10**
Grn. Farm Cl. PE5: Cas 3C **16**
Greengate Ct. PE1: Pet 1C **20**
Greenham PE3: Pet 2C **18**
Green La. PE1: Pet 1A **20**
PE7: Yax 3D **28**
PE9: Stam 2F **7**
Green Man La. PE6: Mar 2A **12**
Green Wlk. PE6: Mkt D 3B **8**
Gresham Sq. PE1: Pet 2E **21**
Gresley Dr. PE9: Stam 5F **7**
Gresley Way PE3: Pet 4E **13**
Gretton Cl. PE2: Pet 6E **19**
Griffiths Ct. PE2: Pet 2A **24**
Grimshaw Rd. PE1: Pet 5B **14**
Grimsthorpe Cl. PE6: Mkt D 3B **8**
Grove, The PE6: Mkt D 3C **8**
PE7: Whit 4E **31**
Grove Ct. PE1: Pet 5H **19**
Grovelands PE1: Pet 3G **19**
Grove La. PE3: Pet 3C **18**
Grove St. PE1: Pet 5H **19**
Guildenburgh Cres. PE7: Whit 3E **31**
Guildhall Wlk. PE1: Pet 4C **4**
Gull Way PE7: Whit 2E **31**
Gullymore PE3: Pet 3B **12**
GUNTHORPE **1G 13**
Gunthorpe Ridings PE4: Pet 6H **11**
Gunthorpe Rd. PE4: Pet 1F **13**
PE6: Newb 6H **11**
Gurnard Leys PE3: Pet 2C **12**
Guthlac Av. PE4: Pet 3F **13**
Gwash Way PE9: Stam 2H **7**

H

Hacke Rd. PE3: Pet 2F **19**
Haddonbrook Bus. Cen. PE2: Pet 5F **23**
Haddon Cl. PE2: Pet 2E **27**
Haddon Rd. PE1: Pet 2G **19**
PE9: Stam 3D **6**
Haddon Way PE7: Far 5B **26**
Hadley Rd. PE4: Pet 2F **13**
Hadrians Ct. PE2: Pet 5B **20**
Halesowen Pl. PE6: Eye 1G **15**
Half Acre Drove PE7: East 3G **31**
Halfleet PE6: Mkt D 2B **8**
Hallaton Rd. PE1: Pet 3D **14**
Hallcroft Rd. PE7: Whit 3B **30**
Hall Farm PE6: Mkt D 2C **8**
Hallfields La. PE4: Pet 1G **13**
Hallidays Yd. *PE9: Stam* *4F* **7**
(off Radcliffe Rd.)
Hall La. PE4: Pet 5E **11**
Hall Mdw. Rd. PE6: Deep J 1G **9**
Hambleton Rd. PE9: Stam 5C **6**
Ham La. PE2: Pet 6H **17**
HAMPTON **4F 25**
HAMPTON CENTRE **5G 25**
Hampton Ct. PE3: Pet 5E **13**
HAMPTON HARGATE **4E 25**
HAMPTON LEYS **5H 25**
HAMPTON VALE **6E 25**
Hanbury PE2: Pet 4B **24**
Hankey St. PE1: Pet 1H **19**
Hannington Cl. PE7: Whit 3F **31**
Hanover Ct. PE3: Pet 3C **12**
PE9: Stam 4G **7**
Harcourt Ter. PE9: Stam 4E **7**
Hardwick Ct. PE3: Pet 3D **18**
Hardwick Rd. PE9: Stam 3D **6**
Hardys La. PE7: Whit 4D **30**
Harebell Cl. PE1: Pet 2B **14**
Harewood Gdns. PE3: Pet 3D **18**
Hargate Way PE7: Pet 5D **24**
Harlech Grange PE3: Pet 4D **18**
Harlton Cl. PE2: Pet 2E **27**
Harn Rd. PE7: Pet 5G **25**
Harpers Cl. PE7: Whit 3C **30**
Harrier Pk. PE2: Pet 5H **23**
Harrison Cl. PE3: Pet 2B **18**
Harris St. PE1: Pet 5H **13**
Hartford Ct. PE2: Pet 1D **26**
Hart's La. PE7: Whit 3C **30**
Hartwell Ct. PE3: Pet 6F **13**
Hartwell Way PE3: Pet 5D **12**
Harvester PE3: Pet 1E **19**
Harvester Way PE1: Pet 4C **20** (4G **5**)
Hastings Rd. PE4: Pet 1E **13**
Havelock Dr. PE2: Pet 1E **27**
Haveswater Cl. PE4: Pet 1G **13**
Hawkshead Way PE4: Pet 6G **11**
Hawthorn Cl. PE6: Mkt D 2C **8**
Hawthorn Dr. PE7: Whit 4E **31**
Hawthorn Rd. PE1: Pet 5C **14**
PE7: Yax 4F **29**
Hayward PE3: Pet 1E **19**
Haywards Fld. PE3: Pet 4C **18**
Hazel Ct. *PE9: Stam* *4F* **7**
(off Radcliffe Rd.)
Hazel Cft. PE4: Pet 5C **10**
Hazel Gro. PE9: Stam 3B **6**
Headlands Way PE7: Whit 2C **30**
Heather Av. PE1: Pet 3A **14**
Heatherdale Cl. PE7: Far 2C **26**
Heath Row PE1: Pet 2B **14**
Heaton Cl. PE3: Pet 2D **18**
Hedgelands PE4: Pet 4E **11**
Helmsdale Gdns. PE4: Pet 1D **12**
Helmsley Ct. PE2: Pet 1F **27**
Helpston Rd. PE5: Ail, Mar 3B **16**
PE6: Ail, Mar 3B **16**
PE6: Glin 1A **10**
Heltwate PE3: Pet 4D **12**
Heltwate Ct. PE3: Pet 4D **12**
Hemingford Cres. PE2: Pet 1E **27**
Hemmerley Dr. PE7: Whit 2D **30**
Hempsted Rd. PE7: Pet 6E **25**
Henry Ct. PE1: Pet 1A **20** (1C **4**)
Henry Penn Wlk. PE1: Pet 6C **4**
Henry St. PE1: Pet 1A **20**
Henshaw PE1: Pet 5E **15**
Hereward Arc. PE1: Pet 3D **4**
Hereward Cl. PE1: Pet 3B **20** (4F **5**)
Hereward Cross PE1: Pet 3A **20** (3D **4**)
Hereward Rd. PE1: Pet 3B **20** (4F **5**)
Hereward Way PE6: Deep J 4F **9**
Heritage Ct. PE1: Pet 6C **14**
Herlington PE2: Pet 3D **24**
Herlington Cen. PE2: Pet 3D **24**
Hermitage, The PE9: Stam 4D **6**
Heron Cl. PE7: Whit 2E **31**
Heron Ct. PE2: Pet 1D **26**
Heron Pk. PE1: Pet 5F **15**
Heronry Dr. PE6: Mar 3A **18**
Herrick Cl. PE1: Pet 3G **13**
Hetley PE2: Pet 3C **24**
Hexham Ct. PE1: Pet 2D **20** (1H **5**)
Heyford Cl. PE4: Pet 1H **13**
Hickling Wlk. PE4: Pet 6G **11**
Hicks La. PE7: Pet 2H **25**
Highbury St. PE1: Pet 6H **13**
High C'way. PE7: Whit 3D **30**
(not continuous)
Highclere Rd. PE7: Pet 4F **25**
High Ct. Way PE7: Pet 1D **28**
Highfield Wlk. PE7: Yax 3G **29**
Highgrove Gdns. PE9: Stam 4C **6**
Highlands Way PE9: Stam 4D **6**
High St. PE2: Pet 1H **25**
PE5: Cas 3D **16**
PE6: Eye 1G **15**
PE6: Glin 1A **10**
PE6: Mkt D 4D **8**
PE9: Stam 4F **7**
High St. St Martin's PE9: Stam 5G **7**
Higney Rd. PE7: Pet 6E **25**
Hillary Cl. PE9: Stam 3H **7**
Hill Cl. PE1: Pet 6D **14**
Hillcrest Av. PE7: Yax 4E **29**
Hillside Wlk. PE7: Yax 3G **29**
Hillward Cl. PE2: Pet 1E **25**
Hinchcliffe PE2: Pet 5A **24**
Hinton Cl. PE7: Whit 2C **30**
Hod Fen Drove PE7: Yax 6E **29**
Hodgson Av. PE4: Pet 3C **10**
Hodgson Cen. PE4: Pet 3D **10**
Hodney Rd. PE6: Eye 1F **15**
(not continuous)
Hog Fen Drove PE7: Yax 4G **29**
Holcroft PE2: Pet 4D **24**
Holdfield PE3: Pet 5D **12**
Holdich St. PE3: Pet 3G **19** (3A **4**)
Holgate La. PE4: Pet 2D **10**
Holkham Rd. PE2: Pet 4H **23**
Holland Av. PE4: Pet 2F **13**
Holland Cl. PE4: Pet 2F **13**
PE6: Mkt D 2B **8**
Holland Rd. PE9: Stam 3G **7**
Holly Wlk. PE7: Pet 4F **25**
Holly Way PE6: Deep J 4E **9**
Holme Cl. PE5: Ail 3B **16**
Holme Rd. PE7: Yax 5E **29**
Holmes Rd. PE6: Glin 2B **10**
Holmes Way PE4: Pet 1G **13**
Holywell Cl. PE3: Pet 4C **18**
Holywell Way PE3: Pet 3B **18**
Home Pasture PE4: Pet 4D **10**
Honey Hill PE4: Pet 2A **14**
Honeysuckle Ct. PE2: Pet 6G **19**
Horsegate PE6: Deep J 4E **9**
PE7: Whit 3C **30**
Horsegate La. PE7: Whit 3C **30**
Horseshoe La. *PE9: Stam* *4F* **7**
(off Sheep Mkt.)
Horseshoe Way PE7: Pet 6F **25**
Horton Wlk. PE3: Pet 6F **13**
Houghton Av. PE2: Pet 2F **27**
Howland PE2: Pet 4C **24**
Hoylake Dr. PE7: Far 2C **26**
Hubberts Ct. PE1: Pet 1F **5**
Humphrys St. PE2: Pet 5F **19**
Hungarton Ct. PE1: Pet 3D **14**
Hunsbury Cl. PE7: Whit 5E **31**
Hunting Av. PE2: Pet 6H **19**
Huntly Gro. PE1: Pet 1A **20**
Huntly Rd. PE2: Pet 6G **19**
Huntly Sq. *PE2: Pet* *3A* **24**
(off Glebe Av.)
Huntsmans Ga. PE3: Pet 2A **18**

Hurn Rd. PE6: Mar 1A 12
  PE6: Pet 5A 10
Hyholmes PE3: Pet 4B 12
Hythegate PE4: Pet 5F 11

I

Ibbott Cl. PE2: Pet 2E 27
Ihlee Cl. PE4: Pet 2G 13
Ilex Cl. PE7: Pet 4E 25
Iliffe Ga. PE4: Pet 1H 13
Illston Pl. PE1: Pet 4E 15
Ingleborough PE1: Pet 6A 14
Inglis Ct. PE3: Pet 2C 12
Inhams Ct. PE7: Whit 4D 30
INHAM'S END 4E 31
Inham's Rd. PE7: Whit 4D 30
Innovation Way PE2: Pet 2F 23
Irchester Pl. PE3: Pet 6F 13
Ireland Ho. PE1: Pet 4E 5
Irnham Rd. PE9: Stam 2G 7
Ironmonger St. PE9: Stam 4G 7
Irving Burgess Cl. PE7: Whit 2B 30
Isham Rd. PE3: Pet 1F 19
Isis Way PE2: Alw 2F 23
Itter Cres. PE4: Pet 2G 13
Ivatt Way PE3: Pet 5E 13
Ivy Gro. PE4: Pet 1F 13
Ivy La. PE7: Whit 3C 30
Ixworth Cl. PE6: Eye 1G 15

J

Jack Hunt Swimming Pool 2D 18
James Gdns. PE7: Whit 3D 30
Jasmine Ct. PE2: Pet 5A 24
Jasmine Way PE7: Yax 3F 29
Jellings Pl. PE1: Pet 1A 20
Joan Wake Cl. PE6: Mkt D 2C 8
John Bird Wlk. PE7: Pet 5C 26
John Eve Way PE6: Mkt D 2C 8
John King Gdns. PE2: Pet 1C 26
Johnson Wlk. PE1: Pet 4H 13
John Wesley Rd. PE4: Pet 6C 10
Jones La. PE7: East 3H 31
Jordan M. PE1: Pet 2B 20 (2E 5)
Jorose Way PE3: Pet 2C 18
Joseph Odam Way PE2: Pet 3F 23
Jubilee Ct. PE3: Pet 4D 12
Jubilee Mans. PE3: Pet 3F 19
Jubilee St. PE2: Pet 5H 19 (6A 4)
Juniper Cres. PE3: Pet 3C 18
Jury Rd. PE7: Pet 1C 28

K

Kariba Ct. PE1: Pet 5H 19
Katharine Way PE3: Pet 6C 12
Keats Gro. PE9: Stam 4C 6
Keats Way PE1: Pet 4G 13
Keble Cl. PE9: Stam 2E 7
Keble Ct. PE9: Stam 2E 7
Kedleston Rd. PE2: Pet 1F 27
Keeton Rd. PE1: Pet 4G 13
Kelful Cl. PE7: East 3H 31
Kelso Ct. PE4: Pet 2E 13
Kendal Cl. PE4: Pet 1H 13
Kendrick Cl. PE2: Pet 1D 26
Kenilworth Av. PE2: Pet 2F 27
Kennels Dr. PE6: Mar 1H 17
Kennet Gdns. PE4: Pet 6G 13
Kentmere Pl. PE4: Pet 1H 13
Kent Rd. PE3: Pet 3G 19 (3A 4)
Kesteven Cl. PE6: Deep J 3D 8
Kesteven Dr. PE6: Mkt D 2B 8
Kesteven Rd. PE9: Stam 2F 7
Kesteven Wlk. PE1: Pet 3B 20 (3E 5)
Kestrel Ct. PE6: Pet 3C 18
Keswick Cl. PE4: Pet 6H 11
Kettering Rd. PE9: Wot, Stam 6F 7
Keyham Ct. PE1: Pet 3G 5
Keys Pk. Mobile Home Pk.
  PE1: Pet 4F 15
Key Theatre & Arts Cen. 4B 20 (6E 5)
Kildare Dr. PE3: Pet 1E 19
Kilham PE2: Pet 5A 24
Kilverstone PE4: Pet 2D 10
Kimbolton Ct. PE1: Pet 2H 19 (1B 4)
Kingfisher Cl. PE7: Yax 3D 28

Kingfisher Rd. PE7: Whit 2E 31
Kingfishers PE2: Pet 1H 23
Kings Acre PE5: Ail 3B 16
Kingsbridge Cen., The PE3: Pet 3E 13
Kingsbridge Ct. PE4: Pet 4C 10
King's Delph PE7: Whit 2H 27
King's Delph Drove PE7: Far 6E 27
King's Delph Highway PE7: Far 5G 27
Kings Dyke Cl. PE2: Pet 1E 27
King's Gdns. PE1: Pet 6A 14
King Henry Chase PE3: Pet 6C 12
Kingsley Rd. PE1: Pet 1C 20 (1H 5)
Kings Mill La. PE9: Stam 5F 7
Kings Rd. PE2: Pet 1B 26
  PE9: Stam 3F 7
Kingston Dr. PE2: Pet 2E 27
KINGSTON PARK 3B 26
King St. PE1: Pet 3H 19 (4C 4)
Kinnears Wlk. PE2: Pet 5B 24
Kipling Cl. PE9: Stam 4C 6
Kipling Ct. PE1: Pet 3G 13
Kirby Wlk. PE3: Pet 1E 19
Kirkmeadow PE3: Pet 3C 12
Kirkstall PE2: Pet 4D 24
Kirkton Ga. PE3: Pet 4C 18
Kirkwood Cl. PE3: Pet 4G 19 (4A 4)
Knight Cl. PE6: Deep J 3E 9
Knighton Cl. PE7: Pet 6F 25
Knights M. PE2: Pet 1A 26
Knole Wlk. PE3: Pet 2D 18

L

Laburnham Gro. PE1: Pet 3B 14
Laburnum Av. PE7: Yax 3F 29
Laburnum Wlk. PE7: Yax 3F 7
Ladybower Way PE4: Pet 6G 11
Lady Charlotte Rd. PE7: Pet 4E 25
Lady Lodge Dr. PE2: Pet 2C 24
Lady Margaret's Av.
  PE6: Deep J, Mkt D 3D 8
Lady Romayne Cl. PE9: Stam 5G 7
Ladysmith Av. PE7: Whit 2E 31
Lakeside PE4: Pet 5F 11
Lakeside Superbowl 3D 4
Lakeview Way PE7: Pet 5E 25
  (not continuous)
Lambert M. PE9: Stam 5G 7
Lambes Ct. PE4: Pet 5C 10
Lambeth Wlk. PE9: Stam 3E 7
Lammas Rd. PE1: Pet 4A 14
Lamport Cl. PE6: Mkt D 2B 8
Lancashire Ga. PE1: Pet 3B 20 (4F 5)
Lancaster Ct. PE7: Yax 3G 29
Lancaster Rd. PE9: Stam 3F 7
Lancaster Wlk. PE7: Yax 3F 29
Lancaster Way PE6: Mkt D 1C 8
  PE7: Yax 3F 29
Lancing Cl. PE4: Pet 6E 11
Landsdowne Rd. PE7: Yax 3F 29
Landy Grn. Way PE5: Cas 5E 17
Langdyke PE1: Pet 5F 15
Langford Rd. PE2: Pet 6A 20
Langley PE3: Pet 3D 12
  (not continuous)
Langton Rd. PE1: Pet 4D 14
Lansdowne Wlk. PE2: Pet 6F 19
Lapwing Dr. PE7: Whit 1F 31
Larch Cl. PE7: Yax 3F 29
Larch Gro. PE1: Pet 5C 14
Larklands PE3: Pet 4D 18
Lark Ri. PE6: Mkt D 3D 8
Larkspur Wlk. PE4: Pet 6F 11
Latham Av. PE2: Pet 1E 26
Lattersey Cl. PE7: Whit 3E 31
LATTERSEY FIELD 4F 31
Lattersey Nature Reserve 5F 31
Launde Gdns. PE9: Stam 5C 6
Laurel Cl. PE7: Yax 5D 28
Lavender Cl. PE7: Yax 3F 29
Lavender Cres. PE1: Pet 3A 14
Lavender Way PE9: Stam 2B 6
Lavenham Ct. PE2: Pet 6E 19
Lavington La. PE7: Pet 5E 15
Lawn Av. PE1: Pet 4A 14
Lawn Cl. PE7: Yax 5E 29
Lawns, The PE4: Pet 2G 13
Lawrence Av. PE7: Far 5C 26
Law's Cl. PE6: Milk N 1H 11
Lawson Av. PE2: Pet 1D 26
Laxton Sq. PE1: Pet 3A 20 (3D 4)

Lazer Force 2D 4
Leading Drove PE7: Yax 6D 28
  (not continuous)
Leaf Av. PE7: Pet 4F 25
Lea Gdns. PE3: Pet 4H 19 (5A 4)
Ledbury Rd. PE3: Pet 2D 18
Ledham PE2: Pet 3H 23
Leeder Cl. PE7: Pet 6D 26
Lee Rd. PE7: Yax 5E 29
Lees, The PE6: Deep J 3F 9
Leeson Ho. PE1: Pet 3B 20 (3E 5)
Leeward Gdns. PE7: Whit 4D 30
Leicester Ter. PE1: Pet 1E 5
Leighton PE2: Pet 3E 23
Leinsters Cl. PE3: Pet 3F 19
Leiston Ct. PE6: Eye 2G 15
Leofric Sq. PE1: Pet 2E 21
Lessingham PE2: Pet 3H 23
Lethbridge Rd. PE4: Pet 1G 13
Levens Wlk. PE3: Pet 2D 18
Lewes Gdns. PE4: Pet 6E 11
Leys, The PE3: Pet 4C 18
Lichfield Av. PE4: Pet 6D 10
Lidgate Cl. PE2: Pet 5E 19
Lilac Rd. PE1: Pet 4C 14
Lilac Wlk. PE7: Yax 3F 29
Lime Kiln Cl. PE1: Pet 1G 19
Limes, The PE5: Cas 4D 16
Lime Tree Av. PE1: Pet 1H 19
  PE6: Mkt D 2B 8
Limetree Cl. PE7: Yax 2F 29
Linchfield Cl. PE6: Deep J 3F 9
Linchfield Rd. PE6: Deep J 1E 9
Lincoln Cl. PE6: Mkt D 2B 8
Lincoln Ct. PE1: Pet 2C 4
Lincoln Ga. PE1: Pet 2A 20 (1C 4)
Lincoln Rd. PE1: Pet 4F 13 (3C 4)
  PE4: Pet 5C 10
  PE6: Deep G 4C 8
  PE6: Glin 1A 10
  PE6: Pet 3B 10
  PE9: Stam 1D 6
Lindens, The PE1: Pet 2A 20 (1C 4)
Lindisfarne Rd. PE6: Eye 2G 15
Lindridge Wlk. PE3: Pet 2C 18
Lindsey Av. PE6: Mkt D 2B 8
Lindsey Cl. PE4: Pet 2F 13
Lindsey Ct. PE6: Deep J 4F 9
Lindsey Rd. PE9: Stam 3G 7
Ling Gth. PE1: Pet 3B 14
Lingwood Pk. PE3: Pet 5C 18
Link Rd. PE1: Pet 2H 19 (1A 4)
Linkside PE3: Pet 2D 12
Linley Rd. PE7: Whit 4D 30
Linnet PE2: Pet 1H 23
Linnet Cl. PE6: Mkt D 3D 8
Lister Rd. PE4: Pet 4H 13
Litchfield Cl. PE7: Yax 4F 29
Lit. Casterton Rd.
  PE9: Lit C, Stam 1D 6
Little Cl. PE6: Eye 2H 15
Lit. Johns Cl. PE3: Pet 2B 18
Littlemeer PE2: Pet 3B 24
Livermore Grn. PE4: Pet 3C 10
Livingstone Rd. PE7: Yax 4D 28
Livingwell Premier Club 5B 10
Lochfyne Cl. PE2: Pet 3F 23
Loch Lomond Way PE2: Pet 3F 23
Locks Cl. PE6: Deep J 5H 9
Loder Av. PE3: Pet 3B 18
Loire Ct. PE1: Pet 1G 19
Lombardy Dr. PE1: Pet 3C 14
London Rd. PE2: Pet 3H 25 (6D 4)
  PE7: Yax, Nor X, Pet 6A 24
London St. PE7: Whit 4C 30
Long C'way. PE1: Pet 3A 20 (4C 4)
Long Drove PE7: Whit 1D 30
Longfield Ga. PE2: Pet 2C 24
Long Pasture PE4: Pet 4D 10
LONGTHORPE 4C 18
Longthorpe Cl. PE3: Pet 3C 18
Longthorpe Grn. PE3: Pet 4D 18
Longthorpe Ho. PE3: Pet 3B 18
Longthorpe Ho. M. PE3: Pet 3B 18
Longthorpe Parkway PE3: Pet 5D 18
Longthorpe Tower 4C 18
Longwater PE2: Pet 1D 24
Lonsdale Rd. PE9: Stam 4C 6
Lord Burghley's Hospital PE9: Stam . . .5G 7
  (off Station Rd.)
Lornas Fld. PE7: Pet 4F 25
Losecoat Cl. PE9: Stam 1H 7

ovells Ct. PE7: Whit 3D **30**
   (off High Causeway)
ow Cross PE7: Whit 2C **30**
owick Gdns. PE3: Pet 6E **13**
owther Gdns. PE4: Pet 1F **13**
oxley PE4: Pet 5C **10**
uddington Rd. PE4: Pet 2F **13**
udlow M. PE3: Pet 3H **19** (4A **4**)
uffenham Cl. PE9: Stam 4C **6**
umby's Ter. PE9: Stam 5G **7**
   (off Water St.)
utton Gro. PE3: Pet 6E **13**
yme Wlk. PE3: Pet 1E **19**
ynch Cotts. PE2: Pet 1G **23**
YNCH WOOD 1G **23**
ynch Wood PE2: Pet 2F **23**
yndale Pk. PE2: Pet 1G **23**
yndon Way PE9: Stam 4C **6**
ynton Rd. PE1: Pet 5H **13**
ythemere PE2: Pet 3E **25**
yvelly Gdns. PE1: Pet 5E **15**

M

lace Rd. PE2: Pet 2D **26**
lcIntyre Ct. PE1: Pet 6C **14**
laffit Rd. PE5: Ail 3B **16**
lagdellan Ct. PE1: Pet 3G **19**
lagee Rd. PE4: Pet 2F **13**
laiden La. PE9: Stam 4G **7**
lain St. PE5: Ail 3B **16**
  PE7: Far 5C **26**
  PE7: Yax 5E **29**
  PE9: Gt Cas 1A **6**
lalborne Way PE2: Pet 4D **24**
lallard Bus. Cen. PE3: Pet 2D **12**
lallard Cl. PE7: Whit 2E **31**
lallard Ct. PE9: Stam 5F **7**
lallard Rd. PE3: Pet 2C **12**
lallory Dr. PE7: Yax 4D **28**
lallory La. PE9: Stam 4F **7**
   (off All Saints St.)
lallory Rd. PE1: Pet 3D **20** (3H **5**)
lalmesbury Dr. PE6: Eye 1H **15**
laltings, The PE9: Stam 5G **7**
   (off Water St.)
  PE9: Wot 6G **7**
lalting Sq. PE7: Yax 3F **29**
laltings Yd. PE9: Stam 5G **7**
lalus Cl. PE7: Pet 4E **25**
lalvern Rd. PE4: Pet 1G **13**
lanasty Rd. PE2: Pet 5H **23**
lancetter Sq. PE4: Pet 2D **12**
landeville PE2: Pet 3B **24**
lanku Cl. PE1: Pet 1F **5**
lanor Av. PE2: Pet 6B **20**
lanor Cl. PE7: Yax 4D **28**
   (not continuous)
lanor Dr. PE4: Pet 6H **11**
lanor Farm La. PE5: Cas 3C **16**
lanor Gdns. PE2: Pet 6C **20**
lanor Gro. Cen., The
  PE1: Pet 2E **21**
lanor Ho. Ct. PE6: Deep J 4F **9**
lanor Ho. St. PE1: Pet 2A **20** (2C **4**)
lanor Leisure Cen. 4D **30**
lanor Vw. PE7: Whit 4C **30**
lanor Way PE6: Deep J 4F **9**
lansfield Ct. PE1: Pet 6C **14**
lanton PE3: Pet 2C **18**
laple Ct. PE7: Yax 3F **29**
laple Gro. PE1: Pet 4B **14**
larconi Dr. PE7: Yax 3D **28**
lardale Gdns. PE4: Pet 1H **13**
larholm Rd. PE3: Pet 2C **12**
  PE4: Pet 2D **12**
  PE5: Cas 4F **17**
  PE6: Cas 3E **17**
larigolds PE6: Deep J 2E **9**
larius Cres. PE7: Pet 4E **25**
MARKET DEEPING 4D **8**
larket Deeping By-Pass
  PE6: Max 4B **8**
  PE6: Mkt D 1B **8**
larket Ga. PE6: Mkt D 4C **8**
larket Pl. PE6: Mkt D 4C **8**
  PE7: Whit 3C **30**
larketstede PE7: Pet 5D **24**

Market St. PE7: Whit 3C **30**
Market Way PE1: Pet 3A **20** (3D **4**)
Markham Retail Pk. PE9: Stam 2H **7**
Marlborough Cl. PE7: Yax 4E **29**
Marlowe Gro. PE4: Pet 3G **13**
Marne Av. PE4: Pet 2E **13**
Marne Rd. PE7: Whit 5E **31**
Marrigold Cl. PE9: Stam 3A **6**
Marriott Cl. PE1: Pet 6E **15**
Marshall's Way PE7: Far 5C **26**
Marsham PE2: Pet 4B **24**
Martin Ct. PE4: Pet 5E **11**
  PE7: Whit 3C **30**
Martin Markham Ind. Est.
  PE9: Stam 2H **7**
Martinsbridge PE1: Pet 4F **15**
Martins Way PE2: Pet 2B **24**
Mary Armyne Rd. PE2: Pet 2D **24**
Mary Walsham Cl. PE2: Pet 2E **27**
Maskew Av. PE1: Pet 4F **13**
Masterton Cl. PE9: Stam 2H **7**
Masterton Rd. PE9: Stam 2G **7**
Matley PE2: Pet 2A **24**
Maud Swift Ct. PE2: Pet 1B **26**
Maxey Cl. PE6: Mkt D 3B **8**
Maxey Vw. PE6: Deep G 5D **8**
Maxwell Rd. PE2: Pet 1F **25**
Mayfield Rd. PE1: Pet 4A **14**
  PE7: East 3H **31**
Mayor's Wlk. PE1: Pet 2H **19** (2A **4**)
  PE3: Pet 2F **19**
Mead, The PE4: Pet 2D **12**
Mead Cl. PE4: Pet 2D **12**
Meadenvale PE1: Pet 5F **15**
Meadow Gro. PE1: Pet 2B **14**
Meadow Rd. PE6: Milk N, Pea 1E **11**
  PE6: Mkt D 3D **8**
Meadows, The PE2: Pet 2B **24**
  PE6: Mkt D 3D **8**
Meadowsweet PE9: Stam 2A **6**
Meadow Vw. PE7: Whit 2D **30**
  PE9: Stam 3H **7**
Meadow Wlk. PE7: Yax 3G **29**
Meadway PE6: Mkt D 2B **8**
Mealsgate PE4: Pet 1H **13**
Medbourne Gdns. PE1: Pet 3D **14**
Medeswell PE2: Pet 3E **25**
   (not continuous)
Medworth PE2: Pet 4B **24**
Meggan Ga. PE3: Pet 4C **18**
Melancholy Wlk. PE9: Stam 5F **7**
Melbourne Rd. PE9: Stam 3H **7**
Melford Cl. PE3: Pet 4C **18**
Mellows Cl. PE1: Pet 2C **20** (2H **5**)
Mellows Ct. PE1: Pet 2C **20** (2H **5**)
Melrose Cl. PE9: Stam 3C **6**
Melrose Dr. PE2: Pet 6A **20**
Mendip Gro. PE4: Pet 1G **13**
Mercian Ct. PE2: Pet 6D **20**
Mere Drove PE7: Yax 5F **29**
Merefield Vw. PE7: Whit 2D **30**
Merelade Gro. PE4: Pet 4C **10**
Mere Vw. PE7: Yax 3G **29**
Mere Vw. Ind. Est. PE7: Yax 3G **29**
Meriton PE2: Pet 4B **24**
Metro Cen., The PE2: Pet 1F **25**
Mewburn PE3: Pet 2C **12**
Meynell Wlk. PE3: Pet 2E **19**
   (not continuous)
Mickle Ga. PE3: Pet 4C **18**
Middlefield PE7: Pet 4F **25**
Middleham Cl. PE2: Pet 2F **27**
Middle Pasture PE4: Pet 4D **10**
Middle Rd. PE6: Newb 1H **11**
Middle St. PE7: Far 5C **26**
Middleton PE3: Pet 1C **18**
Middletons Rd. PE7: Yax 4E **29**
Midgate PE1: Pet 3A **20** (3D **4**)
Midland Rd. PE3: Pet 2G **19** (2A **4**)
Milby Drove PE7: Far 5F **27**
Mildmay Rd. PE4: Pet 3F **13**
Mile Drove PE7: Yax 4H **29**
Milk and Water Drove
  PE7: Far, Pet 3G **27**
MILKING NOOK 1G **11**
Milking Nook Rd. PE6: Milk N 1G **11**
Mill Cres. PE2: Pet 3A **24**
MILLFIELD 6H **13**
Millfield Rd. PE6: Deep J 4F **9**
  PE6: Mkt D 2A **8**
Millfield Way PE7: Whit 4E **31**
   (not continuous)

Mill La. PE7: Alw 2E **23**
  PE8: W New 6A **16**
  PE9: Tin 6B **6**
Mill Rd. PE2: Pet 3A **24**
  PE5: Cas 1D **22**
  PE6: Max 6A **8**
  PE7: Whit 4D **30**
Mill Vw. PE7: Alw 2E **23**
Millwood Gdns. PE3: Pet 3C **18**
Milners Ct. PE9: Stam 4G **7**
   (off Gas St.)
Milnyard Sq. PE2: Pet 5G **23**
Milton Bus. Pk. PE1: Pet 3E **21**
Milton Rd. PE2: Pet 6A **20**
Milton Way PE3: Pet 2A **18**
Mina Cl. PE2: Pet 3D **26**
Minerva Bus. Pk. PE2: Alw 2F **23**
Minster Precincts PE1: Pet ...3A **20** (4D **4**)
Misterton PE2: Pet 4A **24**
Misterton Cl. PE2: Pet 4A **24**
Mitchell Cl. PE7: Yax 3C **20** (4G **5**)
Moggswell La. PE2: Pet 3D **24**
Monarch Av. PE2: Pet 1A **26**
Monks Cl. PE7: Whit 2C **30**
Monks Dr. PE6: Eye 2G **15**
Monks Gro. PE4: Pet 4C **10**
Montague Ho. PE1: Pet 4E **5**
Montagu Rd. PE4: Pet 3F **13**
Montrose Cl. PE9: Stam 3C **6**
Monument Cl. PE1: Pet 1E **5**
Monument St. PE1: Pet 2A **20** (1D **4**)
Moore's La. PE6: Eye 1H **15**
Moorfield Rd. PE3: Pet 2F **19**
Moorhen Rd. PE7: Whit 1E **31**
Moorland Ct. PE4: Pet 5D **10**
Moray Cl. PE9: Stam 3B **6**
Morborne Cl. PE2: Pet 1D **26**
Morborn Rd. PE7: Pet 5E **25**
Moreton's Cl. PE7: Whit 2E **31**
Morgan Cl. PE7: Yax 3E **29**
Morley Way PE2: Pet 2F **25**
Morpeth Cl. PE2: Pet 1E **25**
Morpeth Rd. PE3: Pet 2E **19**
Morris Ct. PE7: Yax 3E **29**
Morris St. PE1: Pet 2B **20** (3F **5**)
Mosel Wlk. PE2: Pet 5G **19**
Moulton Gro. PE3: Pet 5E **13**
Mountbatten Av. PE7: Yax 4E **29**
  PE9: Stam 3E **7**
Mountbatten Way PE3: Pet 5D **12**
  PE7: Whit 4F **31**
Mt. Pleasant PE2: Pet 6C **20**
Mountsteven Av. PE4: Pet 2E **13**
Mountsteven Ho. PE1: Pet 4E **5**
Mowbray Rd. PE6: Pet 2B **12**
Mulberry Cl. PE7: Whit 5E **31**
  PE7: Yax 3G **29**
Mulberry Gdns. PE4: Pet 2G **13**
Muntjac Cl. PE3: Pet 6C **12**
Muskham PE3: Pet 1B **18**
Muswell Rd. PE3: Pet 1G **19**
Myrtle Av. PE1: Pet 4B **14**
Myrtle Ct. PE1: Pet 4C **14**
Myrtle Gro. PE1: Pet 4C **14**
Myrtle Ho. Mobile Home Pk.
  PE1: Pet 6F **15**

N

Nab La. PE4: Pet 2H **13**
Nags Head Pas. PE9: Stam 4G **7**
   (off Ironmonger St.)
Nairn Rd. PE9: Stam 4C **6**
Nansicles Rd. PE2: Pet 1F **25**
Napier Pl. PE2: Pet 1G **23**
Narrow Drove PE7: Yax 4H **29**
Naseby Cl. PE3: Pet 6E **13**
Nathan Cl. PE3: Pet 3C **18**
Neaverson Rd. PE6: Glin 2B **10**
Nelson Pl. PE2: Pet 1E **27**
Nene Cl. PE7: Whit 4D **30**
Nene Ct. PE9: Stam 4E **7**
Nene Parkway PE2: Pet 1D **24**
  PE3: Pet 4B **18**
Nene St. PE1: Pet 3C **20** (3G **5**)
Nene Valley Railway
  Ferry Meadows Station 6A **18**
  Orton Mere Station 6D **18**
  Peterborough Station 4H **19** (6B **4**)
Nene Way PE5: Cas 1F **23**
NETHERTON 2G **19**

NEWARK .6D 14
Newark Av. PE1: Pet 5B 14
Newark Cen., The PE1: Pet 6F 15
Newark Rd. PE1: Pet 6E 15
Newborn Cl. PE2: Pet 2E 27
NEWBOROUGH FEN 3H 11
Newborough Rd. PE4: Pet 1C 14
Newboults La. PE9: Stam 4E 7
Newby Cl. PE3: Pet 2D 18
Newcastle Dr. PE2: Pet 1F 25
Newcomb Ct. PE9: Stam 4F 7
Newcombe Way PE2: Pet 4H 23
New Cross Rd. PE9: Stam 4F 7
NEW ENGLAND 5G 13
New Flame Stadium 5F 7
NEW FLETTON 5H 19
Newgates PE9: Stam 4G 7
Newham Rd. PE9: Stam 2E 7
Newhaven Est. Mobile Home Pk.
  PE7: Whit 2B 30
Newlands Rd. PE7: Whit 1F 31
Newmarket Cl. PE1: Pet 5B 14
New Mdw. Drove PE7: Far 5D 26
New Rd. PE1: Pet 3B 20 (3D 4)
  PE2: Pet 5G 19
    (Earl Spencer Ct.)
  PE2: Pet 3A 24
    (Mill Cres., not continuous)
  PE6: Eye 1H 15
  PE7: Had 6A 24
  PE7: Whit 4D 30
New Row PE6: Deep J 4E 9
New St. PE9: Stam 3G 7
Newton Ct. PE4: Pet 2H 13
Newton Way PE1: Pet 3D 20
NEWTOWN 5H 7
Nicholas Taylor Gdns. PE3: Pet . . .1B 18
Nicholls Av. PE3: Pet 2G 19
Nightingale Ct. PE4: Pet 1A 14
Nightingale Dr. PE7: Yax 3D 28
Nightingales PE6: Mkt D 3D 8
Norburn PE3: Pet 3D 12
Norfolk Sq. PE9: Stam 3F 7
Norfolk St. PE1: Pet 1H 19
Norham Ct. PE2: Pet 2G 27
Norman Cl. PE7: Whit 2D 30
NORMAN CROSS 6A 28
Norman Rd. PE1: Pet 1C 20
Normanton Rd. PE1: Pet 4D 14
North Bank PE1: Pet 4C 20 (5G 5)
Nth. Bank Rd. PE1: Pet 2D 20 (2H 5)
NORTHBOROUGH 6F 9
Northborough Rd. PE6: Milk N 1H 11
Northey Rd. PE6: Pet 2H 21
Nth. Fen Rd. PE6: Glin 1A 10
Northfield Rd. PE1: Pet 4H 13
  PE6: Mkt D 1B 8
NORTHFIELDS 3G 7
Northfields Ct. PE9: Stam 3G 7
Northfields Ind. Est. PE6: Mkt D . . .1D 8
Northgate PE7: Whit 2C 30
Northgate Cl. PE7: Whit 2C 30
Northminster PE1: Pet 2A 20 (2D 4)
North St. PE1: Pet 3A 20 (3C 4)
  PE2: Pet 5C 20
  PE9: Stam 4F 7
North Ter. PE1: Pet 5E 15
Northumberland Av. PE9: Stam 3E 7
Norton Rd. PE1: Pet 5H 13
Norwood La. PE4: Pet 1B 14
  PE6: Pet 1C 14
Norwood La. Cvn. Pk. PE4: Pet . . .1B 14
Nottingham Way PE1: Pet 5C 14
Nursery Cl. PE1: Pet 1A 20
Nursery Gdns. PE7: Whit 4E 31
Nursery La. PE1: Pet 3D 20 (4H 5)

O

Oak Av. PE7: Pet 5D 24
Oakdale Av. PE2: Pet 2D 26
Oakfields PE3: Pet 3C 18
Oak Gro. PE6: Mkt D 3C 8
Oaklands PE1: Pet 1B 20
Oakleaf Rd. PE1: Pet 5C 14
Oakleigh Dr. PE2: Pet 1E 25
Oak Rd. PE6: Glin 1A 10
  PE9: Stam 2B 6
Oak Vw. PE3: Pet 3B 18
Oban Cl. PE9: Stam 3C 6
Occupation Rd. PE1: Pet 5G 13

Odecroft PE3: Pet 4E 13
Odin Cl. PE7: Whit 2D 30
Old Bailey Rd. PE7: Pet 1C 28
Old Barn Pas. PE9: Stam 4F 7
    (off Castle St.)
Oldbrook PE3: Pet 2C 12
Old Ct. M. PE1: Pet 6A 14
Old Crown La. PE7: Whit 3C 30
Oldeamere Way PE7: Whit 4E 31
Oldfield Gdns. PE7: Whit 2C 30
OLD FLETTON 6A 20
Old Gt. North Rd. PE8: W New 6A 16
  PE9: Gt Cas, Stam 1A 6
  PE9: Stam 5G 7
Old Pond La. PE5: Cas 3C 16
Old Priory Farm PE6: Deep J 4G 9
Olive Rd. PE1: Pet 4C 14
Oliver St John Pl. PE3: Pet 3D 18
Orchard, The PE4: Pet 6E 11
  PE6: Mkt D 3C 8
Orchard Cl. PE3: Pet 2F 19
  PE6: Deep J 4E 9
  PE9: Stam 4F 7
Orchard M. PE2: Pet 5H 19
Orchard Rd. PE9: Stam 4F 7
Orchards, The PE2: Pet 3B 24
Orchard St. PE2: Pet 5H 19
  PE7: Whit 3C 30
Orchard Wlk. PE7: Yax 3F 29
Orchid Cl. PE7: Yax 2F 29
Orme Rd. PE3: Pet 1F 19
Orton Av. PE2: Pet 6G 19
ORTON BRIMBLES 2A 24
Orton Cen. PE2: Pet 4A 24
Orton Ent. Cen. PE2: Pet 5G 23
ORTON GOLDHAY 4C 24
ORTON LONGUEVILLE 2B 24
ORTON MALBORNE 3D 24
Orton Mere Station
  Nene Valley Railway 6D 18
ORTON NORTHGATE 3F 23
Orton Parkway PE2: Pet 2H 23
ORTON SOUTHGATE 4A 24
ORTON WATERVILLE 3A 24
ORTON WISTOW 1G 23
Orwell Gro. PE4: Pet 2H 13
Osbourne Cl. PE4: Pet 2H 13
Osbourne Way PE6: Mkt D 3B 8
Osier Av. PE7: Pet 5F 25
Osprey PE2: Pet 5B 24
Osric Ct. PE1: Pet 6C 14
Oswald Rd. PE2: Pet 6F 19
Otago Cl. PE7: Whit 2E 31
Otago Rd. PE7: Whit 2E 31
Otterbrook PE2: Pet 2A 24
Oundle Rd. PE2: Pet 3E 23
  PE7: Alw, Ches 6A 22
  PE8: Elt 6A 22
Outfield PE3: Pet 2C 12
Overstone Ct. PE3: Pet 5E 13
Overton Way PE2: Pet 3B 24
Owl End Wlk. PE7: Yax 4D 28
    (off Kingfisher Cl.)
  PE7: Yax 4D 28
    (Pheasant Way)
Owl's End PE7: Whit 3D 30
Oxburgh Cl. PE2: Pet 2F 27
Oxclose PE3: Pet 3C 12
Oxford Gdns. PE7: Whit 3B 30
Oxford Rd. PE1: Pet 6H 13
  PE9: Stam 2E 7
Oxney Rd. PE1: Pet 6E 15
Oxney Rd. Cvn. Site PE1: Pet 6F 15
Oxney Rd. Ind. Est. PE1: Pet 5F 15

P

Paddock, The PE6: Mkt D 2B 8
  PE9: Stam 4E 7
Paddocks, The PE4: Pet 4C 10
  PE7: Whit 3D 30
Padholme Rd. PE1: Pet 2B 20 (1F 5)
Palace, The 4D 4
Palm Cl. PE1: Pet 3B 14
    (not continuous)
Palmer Cl. PE7: Whit 4E 31
Palmer's Rd. PE1: Pet 6F 15
Palmerston Rd. PE2: Pet 6H 19
Pantiles, The PE1: Pet 1A 20
Panton Cl. PE6: Deep J 3E 9
Papyrus Rd. PE4: Pet 5B 10

Parade, The PE2: Pet 1D 26
Paradise La. PE7: Whit 4C 30
Park Cl. PE7: Yax 4F 29
Park Cres. PE1: Pet 6B 14
Park Dr. PE6: Mkt D 3B 8
Park Est. PE6: Deep J 4F 9
PARK FARM 2F 27
Pk. Farm Cres. PE2: Pet 2F 27
Pk. Farm Rd. PE6: Mar 1H 17
Pk. Farm Way PE2: Pet 2F 27
Pk. Home Av. PE7: Pet 6F 25
Parkinson's La. PE7: Whit 4C 30
Park La. PE1: Pet 2C 20 (1H 5)
  PE7: Whit 3B 30
  PE9: Stam 5G 7
Parkodi Ct. PE1: Pet 1B 20
Park Rd. PE1: Pet 6A 14
    (Millfield)
  PE1: Pet 3A 20 (3C 4)
    (Westgate)
  PE6: Deep J 4E 9
Parkside PE2: Pet 1D 24
Parkside Ter. PE9: Stam 3F 7
    (off Recreation Ground Rd.)
Park St. PE2: Pet 6H 19
Park Ter. PE1: Pet 5A 14
Park Vw. PE9: Stam 5H 7
Parkview Flats PE1: Pet 1B 20
Parliament St. PE1: Pet 6H 13
PARNWELL 4F 15
Parnwell Way PE1: Pet 3F 15
Parslins, The PE6: Deep J 3G 9
Partridge Cl. PE7: Yax 3D 28
Partridge Gro. PE4: Pet 4C 10
PASTON .2A 14
Paston La. PE4: Pet 3F 13
Paston Parkway PE1: Pet 1A 14
  PE4: Pet 4F 11
Paston Ridings PE4: Pet 2G 13
    (not continuous)
Pasture, The PE6: Mkt D 2D 8
Patterdale Dr. PE4: Pet 1A 14
Paulsgrove PE3: Pet 1H 23
Pawlett Cl. PE6: Deep J 3E 9
Paxton Rd. PE7: Pet 3H 23
Paynels PE2: Pet 4C 24
    (not continuous)
Paynesholm PE4: Pet 2A 14
Peacock Sq. PE6: Mkt D 1C 8
Peacock Way PE3: Pet 3B 18
Peake Cl. PE2: Pet 1H 25
Peakirk Rd. PE6: Deep G, N'boro . . .5F 9
  PE6: Glin 1B 10
Pearces Rd. PE6: Pet 6H 15
Pears Ho. PE1: Pet 4E 5
Peartree Wlk. PE7: Yax 3G 29
Peckover Cl. PE2: Pet 2F 27
Peddars Way PE3: Pet 3C 18
Pelham Cl. PE3: Pet 3B 18
Pembroke Av. PE2: Pet 2B 24
Pembroke Gro. PE6: Glin 1B 10
Pembroke Rd. PE9: Stam 2E 7
Pendlebury Dr. PE6: Deep J 3E 9
Pendleton PE3: Pet 5D 12
Pennine Way PE4: Pet 1F 13
Pennington PE2: Pet 4A 24
Penrith Gro. PE4: Pet 1A 14
Pentlands, The PE1: Pet 1G 13
Penyale PE3: Pet 4C 18
Peppercorn Cl. PE1: Pet 5G 13
Percival St. PE1: Pet 3G 19
Peregrine St. PE7: Pet 6F 25
Pernys Cl. PE7: Pet 4F 25
Perth Rd. PE9: Stam 3B 6
PETERBOROUGH 3A 20 (4D 4)
Peterborough Arts Cen. 3B 24
Peterborough Bus. Pk. PE2: Pet . . .2F 23
Peterborough City Rowing Club 4E 19
Peterborough Crematorium PE6: Pet .2B 12
PETERBOROUGH DISTRICT HOSPITAL
  .3G 19 (4A 4)
Peterborough Dr. PE6: Mar 2H 17
Peterborough Embankment Track
  . . . . .4B 20 (5F 5)
Peterborough Lido Swimming Pool
  . . . . .4B 20 (5E 5)
PETERBOROUGH MATERNITY UNIT .3G 19
Peterborough Mus. & Art Gallery . .3H 19 (4B 4)
Peterborough Regional Swimming Pool
  . . . . .3B 20 (4F 5)
Peterborough Rd. PE5: Ail, Cas 3A 16
  PE6: Eye 3E 15